Ysyt

Maya MEL Basics for Designers
First Edition

Nicholas Pisca

Ysyt
Maya MEL Basics for Designers – First Edition

Copyright © 2008

FIRST EDITION: December, 2008

International Standard Book Number:
978-0-578-00988-9

Published by
0001d Publishing
12720 Pacific Ave #9
Los Angeles, CA 90066

Tradmarks

All terms mentioned in this book that are known to be trademarks or service marks have been appropriately capitalized. The publisher and author cannot attest to the accuracy of this information. Use of a term in this book should not be regarded as affecting the validity of the trademark or service mark. Maya is a registered trademark of Autodesk Inc.; Windows is a registered trademark of Microsoft Corporation; Mac is a registered trademark of Apple Inc.

Warning and Disclaimer

This book is designed to provide information about the Maya Embedded Language. Every effort has been made to make this book as complete and as accurate as possible, but no warranty or fitness is implied.

The information is provided on an as-is basis. The author and publisher shall have neither liability nor responsibility to any person or entity with respect to any loss or damage arising from the information contained in this book.

Table of Contents
Introduction and Table of Contents

vi

viii

Thanks to Nathan Engel and Erika Reber.

Chapter 1

Scripting Philosophy
MEL Scripting
Maya User Interface and Files
Basic Maya Navigation
   Zooming
   Panning
   Orbiting
Script Editor Use
History and Input Windows
Saving
Execution and Debugging
Help and the Command Reference
Syntax
Left-to-Right, Semicolons, and Commenting

Scripting Philosophy
Scripting is the use of computer programming language to automate tasks. Computer programming allows users to interact with the application in an extremely efficient mode, utilizing repeated sequences of tasks to accomplish manually-impossible results. Topics such as emergence, evolutionary simulations, topologically-different mutation, breeding optimization, animation expressions, particle systems, and assembly rationalization could not be possible without advanced automation techniques like scripting.

When tasks are "programmed," the computer stores these procedures in text files called scripts. These files are authored by scripters and "executed" by users. In most cases, the user and scripter is the same person. Executing, or "running," is the process of initiating the script, much like a row of stacked dominoes sequentially falls after the first block is toppled. This illustration captures the essence of scripting; preparing a simple but intelligent program for the computer to follow, which requires minimal interaction from the user.

Scripting can be divided into two categories: coding for efficiency and coding for design. "Efficiency codes" consist of simple tasks of automation, used primarily by modelers to alter scene-specific settings, create custom interface features, and ultimately repeat menial tasks. Essentially, these tools increase the speed at which the animator models. Less common, "design codes" consist of the development of tools for effects, form generation, analysis, output, and so on. This field of research is called computational design.

MEL Scripting

The computer programming language used in Maya is called the Maya Embedded Language, often shortened to MEL. For veteran programmers, MEL is similar to C, but does not adhere completely to this language. Coding experience should not be considered a prerequisite for MEL scripting. This book covers the basics of MEL scripting, starting with fundamental programming information and ending with general geometric and rendering automation.

Maya User Interface and Files

The application is designed to enable the modeling and animation of three-dimensional objects. Maya files, called "scenes," save geometry and time data, and the file extensions are ".ma" (Maya Ascii) or ".mb" (Maya Binary). The user interface is comprised of a "viewport" (or quadruple view) surrounded by menu items, icons, tabs and toolbars. The viewport is a perspective visualization that captures the scene from a virtual camera, much like a surveillance camera reports the activities of a targeted space to a monitor. The Menu Interface options are based on a separate pull-down list, where users can choose from *Modeling*, *Animation*, *Dynamics* and *Rendering* workbenches. Bounding the upper portion of the screen, there exist several tabs and icons that cover the manual modeling and animating capabilities of the application. The bottom portion of the interface deals with temporal data, like the timeslider, playback icons and keyframing tools.

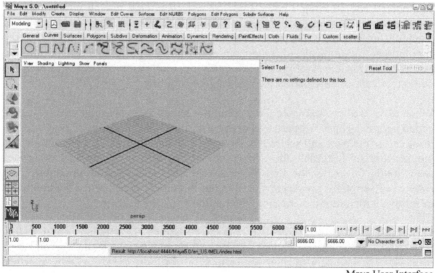

Maya User Interface

Scripts, as stated previously, are text files. Maya has devoted a small portion of the user interface for creating, modifying, running and saving these text files called the Script Editor. Opening the Script Editor is accomplished by clicking on the lowest, right-most icon in the UI or by selecting *Window > General Editors > Script Editor.*

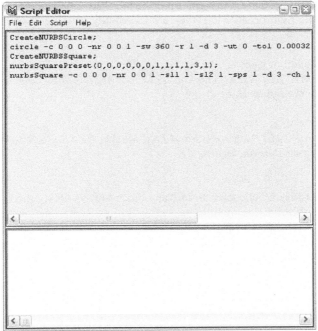

Script Editor Window

Basic Maya Navigation
Technically, scripters can bypass all of the commands built into the user interface via the Script Editor. However there are a few manual tasks that will make viewing the resultant model easier, notably navigation. Navigation is a mouse-controlled process that includes zooming, panning and orbiting. These navigation techniques can be analogized to the movement of a helicopter.
It should be noted, Maya requires a three-button mouse.

Zooming
Zooming in a viewport is similar to the vantage point of an individual piloting a helicopter forward and backward. The aircraft has the capability to fly toward an object, reducing the distance differential, or move away from it.

To zoom in on the model…
*Hold down the "ALT" key, press-and-hold the Right-Mouse Button, and drag the mouse **backward**.*

To zoom out on the model…
*Hold down the "ALT" key, press-and-hold the Right-Mouse Button, and drag the mouse **forward**.*

Panning

Panning is the process of maintaining the same distance and orientation from a target, but shifting to the left, right, up or down. When helicopter pilots ascend, descend, sidle right or sidle left, they are essentially panning in orientation to a target object.

To pan to the left or right...
*Hold down the "ALT" key, press-and-hold the Middle-Mouse Button, and drag the mouse **to the left or right**.*

To pan up or down...
*Hold down the "ALT" key, press-and-hold the Middle-Mouse Button, and drag the mouse **forward or backward**.*

Orbiting

When a pilot flies a helicopter around an object, always facing the target, this is orbiting the object.
To orbit...
*Hold down the "ALT" key, press-and-hold the Left-Mouse Button, and drag the mouse **in any direction**.*

Script Editor Use

The Script Editor allows coders to author their own codes. It holds a series of text editing tools that facilitates the production of MEL scripts. The menu list contains saving tools (File), revision methods (Edit), execution and debugging devices (Script) and language references (Help). The editor is divided vertically to house the History Window (grey) and the Input Window (white).

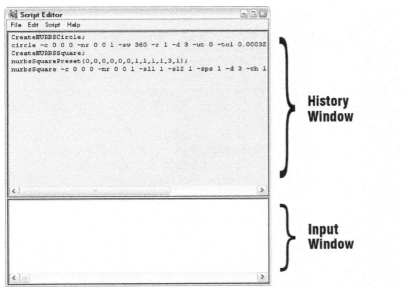

Script Editor History and Input Windows

History and Input Windows

Unlike most other three-dimensional modeling programs, the application developers have provided the means to both author and record scripts. Writing codes is accomplished in the white space on the bottom half of the Script Editor, called the "Input Window." The "History Window" is the grey, top portion of the editor, where most scripted and non-scripted procedures are recorded for future review. This History Window is read-only and the contents can be dragged into the Input Window to efficiently automate.

Saving

MEL scripts are saved as text files with the ".mel" extension. Once a script has been successfully written in the Input Window, there are several means of publishing this code. Saving is very useful, because it allows the scripter to write several codes at once, and publish each group as a separate file.[†] Also, saving codes allows scripters to compile a library of commands over time.

[†] NOTE: Unlike all other program save features, the editor will not save the extension ".mel" when the browser prompts the author. Scripters must save their mel files by writing in the extension following the file name. Forgetting the characters will result in the creation of a file, but it will be extension-less, and can be appended manually later.

These files can be shared with other scripters, as well as be utilized on future projects.

To save the current status of the code...
Select the desired portion of text and click "File" > "Save Selected..."

These codes can be saved as an icon in the current tab in Maya. When saving to an icon, it is imperative that the icon name not exceed five characters. Names should be concise and didactic. An example of a poorly named function is *"CreateSphereBox,"* because the interface will only display the characters *"Creat."* The word *"SphBx"* may be a wiser name.

To save the current status of the code to the application's interface...
Select the desired portion of text and click "File" > "Save Selected to Shelf..."

A previously saved code can be opened or sourced. Opening the file just appends the contents of the Input Window with the browsed MEL script. Sourcing the code will execute it on the current model and place the resultant recorded text in the History Window. Sourcing does not add the text to the input editor.

To add an existing MEL script to the Input Window...
File > Open Script...

To run an existing MEL script on the current file...
File > Source Script...

Execution and Debugging
In addition to sourcing and icon activation of scripts, users can run codes from the Input Window. This is the most widespread script execution method, especially considering that it is common practice to have several codes being authored simultaneously in the same editor.

To run the contents of the Input Window...
Script > Execute
Or
Simultaneously press the keys "CTRL" and "ENTER."

This will clear the contents of the Input Window, run the code and record the text in the History Window. Automatically clearing this text from the Input Window is typically problematic for several reasons: most codes are "in-progress," the user is trying to run single lines for debugging purposes, there exists other codes above and below the current script in the Input Window, et cetera. Just for these reasons, there exists a procedure for running portions of the editor text, without automatically erasing it.

To run only a portion of the Input Window contents...

Select the desired script text and simultaneously press the keys "CTRL" and "ENTER."

Help and the Command Reference
When travelers explore a foreign country, they must gain familiarity with the native language. With practice, foreigners gradually expand their vocabulary and become fluent. Similar to spoken languages, MEL (the Maya Embedded *Language*) is a narrow linguistic apparatus with questions, commands, comments, responses, and so on.

The developers anticipated this language barrier and provided a "command reference." Command references are to computer programming as dictionaries are to spoken languages. Just like dictionaries, command references do not inform the scripter on the composition of the code, but instead provide terms, definitions and variations of use. These references are categorized into alphabet order and by subject.

To open the Command Reference…
Click on the menu item "Help" > "MEL Command Reference…"

Dictionaries have an esoteric structure to each definition; command references follow suit. The typical definition begins with the proper spelling, pronunciation, variants and definition. Some words will have contextual examples to clarify its use. Each command in the reference has similar characteristics.

All command definitions follow this categorical format:
Synopsis:	The proper character syntax of the statement.
ReturnValue:	The names of the objects
Description:	The definition of the command
Flags:	Characteristics of the command
Examples:	Contextual cases
Related Commands:	Words of associative importance

As with all languages, phrases and axioms have a tendancy to lose meaning in translation. Programming languages cannot avoid this tendancy. With experience and manuals like this, coders will become fluent with the scripting language. MEL becomes second nature and time spent studying the command reference will lessen. (*Once a scripter dreams in MEL, they should feel confident with their understanding of the language.*)

Syntax
Learning new words is not enough to be considered fluent; syntax plays an equally important role. Much like the construction of a sentence requires an initial capitalized character, properly-placed punctuation and spaces delimiting words, scripts necessitate particular syntax requirements as well.

Left-to-Right, Commenting and Syntactical Characters

Much like most Western languages, a multi-line MEL code is read from top-to-bottom and, at each line, read from left-to-right. When the application breaks down the code, it cannot skip ahead or skim the content; it will use the characters at the beginning of a line to prepare itself for storing different types of information.

If a user wishes to write informational text in the code, without impacting its procedural aspects, they can add "comments." These comments are usually short sentences explaining that particular portion of code. Using backslash characters (//) , all keys following on that line will be ignored by the application. For multi-line commenting, encapsulate the code with "/*" and end with "*/". Most resultant History Window reporting is surrounded by backslashes.

Because MEL is strikingly similar to C, there are several symbols used to differentiate variables, commands, loops and conditionals. Dollar signs precede variables, brackets follow arrays, parentheses surround conditionals and calculations, braces enclose cases, and backticks encapsulated returning commands, just to name a few. The most common mistake in all MEL scripting is the syntactical line-ender, the semicolon. Even veteran programmers miss this easily-forgetable symbol, which always leads to enigmatic error messages. This manual will explain all of the circumstances regarding syntax characters in subsequent chapters.

Chapter 2

Numerical Variables
Declaring Singular Data-Types
>**Integers**
>**Floats**
Large Values in Floats
Declaring Multiple Data-Types
>**Arrays**
>**Matrices**
>**Vectors**
Redeclaration of Vector, Integer and Float Data-Types
Redeclaration and Substitution of Singular and Array Data-Types

Numerical Variables
Variables allow the user to hold onto data. Depending upon the limitations of the information, variables can be accessed and used in place of a static scalar value. To visualize this, scripted variables are strikingly similar to algebraic variables, with minor deviations.

All computational variables must be categorized by their types, called "data-types." This chapter will only focus on numerical data-types and following chapters will expand onto character variables. It is imperative that these distinctions are pre-determined, because the computer cannot store conflicting data-types. Pre-determining variables is called "declaring," and once a variable is established, it cannot be redeclared.

Lastly, variables can be stored singularly or collectively. There are two singular numerical data-types: integers and floats. These consist of whole numbers (any positive or negative non-decimal value) and real numbers (any positive or negative decimal value), respectively. There exist three multi-value variables: arrays, matrices and vectors. Vectors, arrays and matrices are just lists of other data-types. Multi-value variables offer the convenience of holding onto several different values with one name.

Variables are the computational equivalent of mailboxes. Like mailboxes, variables can be empty or full. When a user declares a variable, its default state is to be empty, or "nothing," which by definition equals zero with numerical data-types. The user can immediately replace the empty value with a number or leave the variable in its default state. At any point in the scripting process, this variable can have its contents replaced with a compatible value, and conversely, its contents cleared. All variables begin with the character "$" and are case-sensitive.

Declaring Singular Data-Types
Integers
The most basic variable is the Integer. Integers are whole numbers—any positive or negative non-decimal value.

```
-23
0
34319
```

To declare an integer, use the abbreviation "int." The variable name, preceded by "$," can be any string of alphabetic characters and underscores. The first character must be a letter.

```
int $SampleInt;
```

A scripter might ask, *"Why declare a variable without assigning it?"* This is to secure this variable data-type for future debugging. If the user has reserved this variable name for just integers, no other type is allowed, resulting in informative warnings from the application.

To declare an integer with a non-default initial value, assign the value directly:

```
int $SampleInt2 = 55;
int $SampleInt3 = -2322;
```

At any point in the code, a scripter can reassign the current value of the variable. Note the declaration of the integer only occurs with the first instance of the variable name.

```
int $SampleInt4 = 100;
$SampleInt4 = -200;
$SampleInt4 = 300;
```

Integers cannot have decimal information. If the variable has been declared prior to assignment, the digits to the right of the decimal place will be removed. This is called "truncating." For "rounding," see the chapter on Mathematics.

```
int $SampleInt5 = 300.992;
```

In the History Window…

```
// Result: 300 //
```

Floats
Floats, or floating point numbers, are real numbers—any positive or negative decimal value.

```
-23.666
0.0
34319.1028
```

To declare a float, use the term "float."

```
float $SampleFloat;
```

To declare a float with a non-default initial value, assign the value directly:

```
float $SampleFloat2 = 55.667;
float $SampleFloat3 = -2322.0;
```

As with integers, floats can be reassigned at any point.

```
float $SampleFloat4 = 100.1;
$SampleFloat4 = -200.2;
$SampleFloat4 = 300.3;
```

Floats can store whole number information, but it is a best practice to add the decimal data.

```
float $SampleFloat5 = 300.0;
```

In the History Window...

```
// Result: 300 //
```

Since floats store more digits than integers, inappropriately declaring numbers can slow the code or be expensive, memory-wise. The computers memory is similar to a financial budget; spend too much on "expensive" variables and the code will eventually deplete its resources. It is best to reserve whole number assignments to integers as much as possible.

Large Values in Floats
MEL has a tendency to return incorrect information when inputting a large number. When using numbers greater than one billion, use scientific notation.

Incorrect assignment: (Note, the result is a useless "-1")

```
float $HH = 9999999999;
// Result: -1 //
```

Correct scientific assigning:

```
float $HH = 9.99e+009;
// Result: 9990000000 //
```

Declaring Multiple Data-Types
Arrays
Often a scripter wants to store several bits of data simultaneously, but not require the creation of several integer or float variable names. This is common when the count is unknown, large and/or a combination of the two. These lists of values can be extracted by querying an "index" of the collection.

A user can make a list of floats, integers, and, as will be stated in later chapters, characters (named strings). These arrays cannot mix different data-types, so the list must be populated with same types. Declaration of an array appears similar to the singular variables, but with the addition of the bracket characters "[]"

```
int $SampleIntArr[];
float $SampleFloatArr[];
```

An unassigned, unset array will have a "size" of zero. Size and assignments are two different concepts: *size* pertains to the number of elements in the list and *assignments* are the values of the elements.

```
int $SampleIntArr2[5];
float $SampleFloatArr2[18];
```

The aforementioned declarations are still unassigned, but have been set. $SampleIntArr2 still has no values stored in it, but it is now limited to a count of six integer elements. $SampleFloatArr2 is restricted to nineteen floating point elements. All arrays begin with zero, so setting a restriction to the size is always one less than the actual count.

Loading values into an array requires the use of braces "{}." As long as the data-types match, all elements can be delimited by commas.

```
int $SampleIntArr3[] = {66, -2, 0, 201};
float $SampleFloatArr3[] = {-1.0, 2.667, 23887.1};
```

In the History Window…

```
// Result: 66 -2 0 201 //
// Result: -1 2.667 23887.1 //
```

Storing arrays always results in lists separated by spaces. This is useful when operating on several objects, which will be discussed in later chapters.
v
Arrays can also have one element. This is still considered a list, even though the population is a singular value.

```
float $SampleFloatArr3[] = {23887.1};
```

To the non-programmer, retrieving elements from an array requires a counter-intuitive sequence. Computers tend to begin with zero, and not one. So counting begins...

0, 1, 2, 3, 4, 5, 6, 7, 8, 9, 10, 11...

For a five element list, the indices would correspond to...

```
//                          0    1     2      3    4
float $SampleFloatArr3[] = {-1.0, 2.667, 2387.1, 2.1, 1};
```

To extract a specific index, the scripter needs only to place the respective whole number in the brackets of the variable name.[‡]

```
print $SampleFloatArr3[0];
// Result: -1 //
print $SampleFloatArr3[1];
// Result: 2.667 //
print $SampleFloatArr3[2];
// Result: 2387.1 //
print $SampleFloatArr3[3];
// Result: 2.1 //
print $SampleFloatArr3[4];
// Result: 1 //
```

A user can copy an array by extracting values into singular variables. These singular variables must match data-types. If not, integers will truncate the float array values.

```
float $SampleFloatArr3[] = {-1.0, 2.667, 2387.1, 2.1, 1};

float $FirstFloat = $SampleFloatArr3[0];
// Result: -1 //
float $SecondFloat = $SampleFloatArr3[1];
// Result: 2.667 //
float $ThirdFloat = $SampleFloatArr3[2];
// Result: 2387.1 //
float $FourthFloat = $SampleFloatArr3[3];
// Result: 2.1 //
float $FifthFloat = $SampleFloatArr3[4];
// Result: 1 //
```

Integer arrays can also be broken down as well.

```
int $SampleIntArr3[] = {-1, 2, 2387, 2, 1};

int $FirstInt = $SampleIntArr3[0];
// Result: -1 //
int $SecondInt = $SampleIntArr3[1];
```

[‡] The following examples use the command "print" which will be explained in later chapters. In brief, this command reports the value stored in a variable, by printing it in the History Window.

```
// Result: 2 //
int $ThirdInt = $SampleIntArr3[2];
// Result: 2387 //
int $FourthInt = $SampleIntArr3[3];
// Result: 2 //
int $FifthInt = $SampleIntArr3[4];
// Result: 1 //
```

The previous examples copied the array numbers into dedicated float or int variables in order. Users are not limited to extracting data in order; a single element or group of elements in an array can be extract anywhere in the array at any time in the process of the code.

Matrices
Matrices are variables which add another dimension to the concept of an array. While arrays hold onto linearly-ordered elements, matrices retain a grid of elements. One can look to spreadsheets as a good way to describe how a matrix is numbered. Spreadsheets are a table with numbers and letters denoting the rows and columns, respectively. The same can be said about matrices, but columns and rows are labeled with numerical indices.

Like array, the bracket characters denote the matrix data-type. The distinct difference is that two sets of brackets are required, i.e.:

```
matrix $MatrixName[a][b];
```

The declaration requires the word "matrix" preceding the variable. Characters "[a]" stands for the row number, while the second index "[b]" pertains to the column.

```
matrix $TestMat[4][5] = <<77.0, 0.0, 99.1, 0.02, 1001;
                         -1.0, 2.0, -3.0, 4.90, 88.0;
                         23.0, -9.1, -0.3, 1.1, 9.9;
                          5.23, 6.19, 1.0, 77.0, 43.0  >>;
```

```
// Result: << 77 0 99.1 0.02 1001;   -1 2 -3 4.9 88;   23 -9.1 -
0.3 1.1 9.9;   5.23 6.19 1 77 43 >> //
```

Vectors
The most unique data-type in MEL is the vector. As in physics and mathematics, vectors correspond to an X, Y and Z dimension in space. Vectors are non-resizable three-value floats. The syntax for vector declaration is as follows:

```
float $SampleVector1 = <<5.2, 2.2, -1.7>>;
// Result: <<5.2, 2.2, -1.7>>  //
```

Returning the X, Y or Z values from a vector is substantially different than a three-member array. The syntax requires the name of the vector and the desired directionality, separated by a period. The first index uses the character "x," the second index uses "y" and the last uses "z." Additionally, the vector-plus-direction text must be encapsulated with parentheses, or errors will occur.

```
print ($SampleVector1.x);
// Result: 5.2  //
```

The same criteria applies to the Y and Z directions.

```
print ($SampleVector1.y);
// Result: 2.2  //
print ($SampleVector1.z);
// Result: -1.7  //
```

Vectors, like small arrays, can also be split apart into singular variables. This is useful when the scripter just wants to dedicate a separate variable for the X, Y or Z coordinates of a converted vector. Since all vectors use by default three floating point values, extracting numbers from an existing vector requires a float data-type.

```
float $SampleVector1 = <<5.2, 2.2, -1.7>>;

float $FirstVecVal = ($SampleVector1.x);
// Result: 5.2 //
float $SecondVecVal = ($SampleVector1.y);
// Result: 2.2 //
float $ThirdVecVal = ($SampleVector1.z);
// Result: -1.7 //
```

Redeclaration of Vector, Integer and Float Data-Types
Once a variable has been declared and executed, the variable name is stored in the memory with the specified data-type until the application is closed. There is no way to replace or "redeclare" the data-type from an integer to a float, float to a vector, or vector to an integer.

Valid float declaration and assignment:

```
float $Var19 = 2300.0;
// Result: 2300 //
```

Incorrect redeclaration from a float to an int:

```
int $Var19 = 2300;
// Error: int $Var19 = 2300; //
// Error: Line 1.12: Invalid redeclaration of variable "$Var19"
as a different type. //
```

Redeclaration is a common error when working collaboratively. Often scripters tend to use the same name for similar variables however their data-types may differ. The only way to clear the variables is to restart the application or rename it. Renaming is problematic in lengthy codes because the scripter must find all instances of that name and replace it with the new word.

When working together on a project, separate coders should prefix their variable names with an abbreviation. Then if when the codes are combined, there are no conflicts. In the example below, Veronica and Mike add the characters "V" and "M" before their variables:

```
float $V_Var19 = 2300.0;
// Result: 2300 //
int $M_Var19 = 2300;
// Result: 2300 //
```

Redeclaration and Substitution of Singular and Array Data-Types
An *integer* variable may appear to be the same as an *integer array* variable, but this is deceptive. The elements of an *integer array* are *integers*, but the array is a different type than the singular variable. If a variable has been declared as an array, regardless of the type of array, this variable cannot be redeclared as any other data-type or non-array.

Valid float array declaration and assignment:

```
float $SampleVar20[] = {2.1, 5.1, -0.1};
// Result: 2.1 5.1 -0.1 //
```

Incorrect redeclaration from a float array to a float:

```
float $SampleVar20 = 33.0;
// Error: float $SampleVar20 = 33.0; //
// Error: Line 1.20: Invalid redeclaration of variable
"$SampleVar20" as a different type. //
```

In the example above, the user cannot change the array to a single value. If the intent was to replace an index of the array, the scripter should specify the element and substitute it directly:

```
$SampleVar20[1] = 33.0;
// Result: 33 //
print $SampleVar20;
```

Result: *2.1 33.0 -0.1*

Chapter 3

Mathematics and Conditions
Arithmetic and Algebraic Operations
>**Non-Decimal Float Assignments**
>**Order of Operations**
>**Parentheses**
>**Math Commands**
>**Trigonometric Commands**
>**Vector Commands**
>**Scripting Commands**

Logic
>**Conditional Syntax**
>**Operators**
>**Greater/Less Than (and Equal to)**
>**Equal Value Tests**
>**"Is-Equal-to" versus "Equal-to"**
>**And/Or Gates**
>**Typical Gate Scenarios**
>**Extra Conditional Tests**

Mathematics and Conditionals
With all computational design, mathematics and logic are the cornerstones of programming. Mathematical commands give programmers the ability to solve batch calculations, and logic operators allow for projects to be infused with deterministic intelligence. At first glance, these tools appear to be basic and rudimentary. However, when correctly utilized and nested, logic statements and math will exponentially increase the intelligence of the script.

The list of mathematical commands can be divided into three main groups. The first family of mathematical tools are standard arithmetic operations, like addition, multiplication, etc. The second subset consists of trigonometric methods and the last group is specialized for computer programming arithmetic. Nearly all of the math topics in the MEL language are translations from basic high-school mathematics. Though more advanced mathematical knowledge always is optimal, a basic pre-calculus math background is sufficient for the typical scripter.

Logical statements, also called conditionals, return values in terms of true or false. This structure allows scripts to make decisions based on changing data. Conditionals can be a direct analysis between two values or a combination of values calculations through what are called "gates."

Arithmetic and Algebraic Operators

With most programming languages, the four standard mathematical symbols are as follows:

Addition: +
Subtraction: –
Multiplication: *
Division: /

```
float $HD = 2.0 + 3.0;
// Result: 5 //
float $HD = 2.0 - 3.0;
// Result: -1 //
float $HD = 2.0 * 3.0;
// Result: 6 //
float $HD = 2.0 / 3.0;
// Result: 0.666667 //
```

Mathematical impossibilities result in computational errors. These warnings will stop the code at the instance of the error.

```
float $HD = 2.0 / 0;
// Error: line 1: Division by zero. //
```

Non-Decimal Float Assignments
When a scripter uses integers in the equation, the overall output of the value will hold that conversion. Numerical integers are any series of digits without a decimal point. In the example below, the integers "2" and "3" will truncate the resultant value of 0.666667 to 0.

Incorrect float calculation:

```
float $HD = 2 / 3;
// Result: 0 //
```

Correct float calculation:

```
float $HD = 2.0 / 3.0;
// Result: 0.666667 //
```

Order of Operations
With all arithmetic calculations, the order of operations is paramount. When the application finds a variable assignment where math is involved, it begins to solve the equation from the left to the right. Whenever it finds a multiplication or division sign, these characters take precedence over addition and subtraction

```
float $HD = 6 * 2 - 2;
// Result: 10 //
```

```
float $HD = 2 - 2 * 6;
// Result: -10 //
```

Parentheses

Since the application reads the equation from left-to-right, parentheses are often needed to encapsulate preliminary results. The program calculates the from the inner-most parentheses first and works outward. There is no limit to the number of parentheses combinations to an equation, but remember to always "end parentheses" or errors will result.

```
float $HD = (6 * 2) - 2;
// Result: 10 //
float $HD = 6 * (2 - 2);
// Result: 0 //
float $HD = (2 - 2) * 6;
// Result: 0 //
float $HD = 2 - (2 * 6);
// Result: -10 //
```

Math Commands

Unlike arithmetic operators, most other mathematical topics do not have a dedicated character like + or *. The remainder of the math tools will be in a command format. There exists an entire library of math commands, each with their own float, integer or vector input data.

```
abs
ceil
cos
cross
crossProduct
deg_to_rad
dot
dotProduct
exp
log
mag
max
min
pow
rad_to_deg
rand
sin
sqrt
tan
unit
```

Single input math functions are very basic. The command is followed by parentheses encapsulating the variable or number. An example of a single input is "abs()" which stands for the absolute value.

```
float $HTVal = abs(-23.0);
// Result: 23 //
```

Most math functions require two or more inputs. Separate inputs are separated with commas, and in most cases, do not follow the same syntax as typical high school math. A good example of the difference between computational math syntax and standard math is the use of the command "pow," which calculates exponential values.

Raising a value to a power typically looks like this: 3^4 However, programming languages do not allow for superscript characters.

Using a command to accomplish the same calculation looks like this:

```
float $EPNum = pow(3, 4);
// Result: 81 //
```

Trigonometric Commands
When programming with trig functions, units are vital. MEL remembers all angle calculations with radians, which is counter to the applications degree constraint angles. Some of the main trigonometric functions are…

```
cos
sin
tan
deg_to_rad
rad_to_deg
```

Vector Commands
Some calculations require the use of vectors. To review, vectors are variables that contain three float numbers. These values correspond to the standard (x, y, z) coordinate format.

```
cross
crossProduct
dot
dotProduct
mag
unit
```

Some vector commands return vector data, while others return basic real numbers. The command "mag" returns the length of a vector, or in other words the distance between the vector coordinate (x_1, y_1, z_1) and the origin (0, 0, 0).

```
vector $JVec = <<5.2, 8.1, -1.0>>;
float $JVecLen = mag($JVec);
// Result: 9.677293 //
```

An example of a vector output command is "unit." This command takes an input vector and produces a vector with the same orientation at a limited length of one unit. The unit vector is a useful mechanism for calculating the orientation of an object, which will be covered in later chapters.

```
vector $JVec = <<5.2, 8.1, -1.0>>;
vector $JUnit = unit($JVec);
// Result: <<0.53734, 0.837011, -0.103335>>  //
```

Logic
Conditional Syntax

As stated in the introduction to this chapter, conditionals control the intelligence of a script. They return true or false statements, called Booleans, based on simple mathematical conclusions. Conditionals are like gatekeepers—if asked a question and the answer is true, the gatekeeper opens up part of the code.

Using proper syntax, conditionals are broken into three parts. The first sets up the Boolean with the characters "if," the second encapsulates the logical operation with parentheses, and the last is a reservation code surrounded by braces, "{}". In the example below, the statement is "(2 < 3)." In this particular case, two is less than three, so the result of the conditional is true, opening up the code in the braces.

```
if (2 < 3) {
     print "OK.";
}
```

Result: *"OK."*

In this example, two is not greater than three, so the portion of code within the braces is locked out. These lines are skipped.

```
if (2 > 3) {
     print "OK.";
}
```

Result: *Nothing*

The previous examples showed how a simple conditional can either give access to a braced-encapsulated portion of code, or just simply deny access. The following example shows how conditionals can have more than one option. If true, the code prints "Less Than." If false, the code prints "Greater Than." The If/Else conditional is the most common Boolean operation in computer programming

```
if (2 < 3) {
     print "Less Than.";
}
else {
     print "Greater Than.";
}
```

Result: *"Less Than."*

These examples have not been very useful. It is evidently clear two is always less than three. However, as stated in the previous chapter, any static numerical value can be replaced with a float or integer variable. If we declare dedicated variables for the conditional test, these numbers can fluctuate and result in differing outcomes.

```
float $x = 12.0;
float $y = 3.0;
if ($x < $y) {
        print "Less Than.";
}
else {
        print "Greater Than.";
}
```

Result: *"Greater Than."*

Operators
All conditionals are testing between two values. There exist six typical mathematical operator tests that give varying degrees of accessibility.

```
<
>
<=
>=
==
!=
```

Greater/Less Than (and Equal to)
Most conditionals are designed to toggle between ranges of values. Scripters do not want to know all of the possible combinations of potential outcomes, but whether values fall before or after a specific variable. This is accomplished by determining relative numerical relationships with the following configurations:

1.) ($x < $y)   ...is less than...
2.) ($x > $y)   ...is greater than...
3.) ($x <= $y)   ...is less than and equal to...
4.) ($x >= $y)   ...is greater than and equal to...

```
float $x = 12.0;
float $y = 3.0;
if ($x <= $y) {
        print "Less Than.";
}
else {
        print "Greater Than.";
}
```

Result: *"Greater Than."*

Equal Value Tests
The reference has provided two ways to check exact values. The first returns a Boolean if values are identical, in other words equal, and vis-versa for unequal scenarios. Tests of equality are useful for cases when programming requires precision. Also, equality conditionals are important for the beginning and end of a sequence. First and last components of a system usually require additional lines of code.

5.) ($x == $y)   ...is equal to...
6.) ($x != $y)   ...is not equal to...

"Is Equal to" Example:

```
float $x = 3.0;
float $y = 3.0;
if ($x == $y) {
      print "Equal to.";
}
else {
      print "Not Equal to.";
}
```

Result: *"Equal to."*

"Is Not Equal to" Example:

```
float $x = 8.0;
float $y = 3.0;
if ($x != $y) {
      print "Not Equal to.";
}
else {
      print "Equal to.";
}
```

Result: *"No Equal to."*

"Is-Equal-to" versus "Equal-to"
The test "is equal to" is vastly different than "equal to." When there exists two consecutive equal signs, this pertains to a conditional test. When only one equal sign is used, this deals with variable assignments. Mixing these concepts will always result in errors which will halt the code.

Incorrect Equals Sign Syntax.
Variable assigning should not use "is equal to" (==),

```
float $x == 12.0;
float $y == 3.0;
```

```
// Error: float $x == 12.0;
// Error: Line 1.11: Syntax error //
// Error: float $y == 3.0;
// Error: Line 2.11: Syntax error //
```

and conditional tests should not have single equal sign syntax (=).

```
if ($x = $y) {
        print "Equal to.";
}
```

```
// Error: Line 1.7: Syntax error //
```

Correct Equals Sign Syntax:

```
float $x = 12.0;
float $y = 3.0;
if ($x == $y) {
        print "Equal to.";
}
```

And/Or Gates
Gates are logical ways of combining basic conditional tests. Unlike other programming languages which may have several gates, MEL only has two: "And" or "Or."

```
&&      (And)
||      (Or)
```

When using "And" gates, this will verify if and only if both conditions are satisfied. If at least one condition is false, then all is false. "Or" gates test if at least one of the conditions is satisfied. The "Or" operator is two consecutive "bar" or "pipe" characters; this can be found on a standard Qwerty keyboard underneath the "Backspace."

"And" Example 1 (only one case satisfied):

```
float $x = 12.0;
float $y = 3.0;

if ($x > 8.0 && $y > 8.0) {
        print "Both Greater Than.";
}
```

Result: *Nothing*

"And" Example 2 (both cases satisfied):

```
float $x = 12.0;
float $y = 9.0;
```

```
if ($x > 8.0 && $y > 8.0) {
        print "Both Greater Than.";
}
```

Result: *"Both Greater Than."*

"Or" Example 1 (No cases satisfied):

```
float $x = 4.0;
float $y = 3.0;

if ($x > 8.0 || $y > 8.0) {
        print "Accessed Portion.";
}
```

Result: *Nothing*

"Or" Example 2 (One case satisfied):

```
float $x = 12.0;
float $y = 7.0;

if ($x > 8.0 || $y > 8.0) {
        print "Accessed Portion.";
}
```

Result: *"Accessed Portion."*

Typical Gate Scenarios
Since the application reads from left to right, there exist several seemingly simple mathematical tests that must be converted for programming style. For example:

If a user wants to determine if 3 < x < 45,

Incorrect Syntax:

```
float $x = 12.0;
if (3 < $x < 45) {
        print "OK.";
}
```

Correct Syntax:

```
float $x = 12.0;
if ($x > 3.0 && $x > 45.0) {
        print "OK.";
}
```

Result: *"OK."*

Extra Conditional Tests
For all of the aforementioned conditional tests, there exist one or two possible solutions. The implication is if the test is true, the script unlocks the upper portion of brace-encapsulated, or if false, it opens the post-"else" portion of embraced code. This is a bit of an illusion; the word "else" should be redefined. A better description is to equate the word "else" to "if no other test is satisfied, default to here."

Currently, this chapter has limited conditional testing to single cases, but programmers often need to work with several possible outcomes. A good way to visualize this is to think of a postman as the person processing the conditional. As he approaches an apartment building, the number on the door is the test. If the letter's address matches the door, it is placed in the respective slot. If no apartment in the complex corresponds to the address, then this package is returned to the post office.

This sort of logic cannot be scripted with just one test. To infuse the project with more logic, the words "else if" will add alternative tests.

```
float $AptNumber = 4;

if ($AptNumber == 1) {
       print "Mr. Frazer";
}
else if ($AptNumber == 2) {
       print "Mr. Sims";
}
else if ($AptNumber == 3) {
       print "Mr. Csuri";
}
else if ($AptNumber == 4) {
       print "Mr. Reynolds";
}
else if ($AptNumber == 5) {
       print "Mr. Novak";
}
else if ($AptNumber == 6) {
       print "Mr. Chu";
}
else if ($AptNumber == 7) {
       print "Mr. Pisca";
}
else {
       print "Return to Sender";
}
```

Result: *"Mr. Reynolds."*

If in the previous example the variable $AptNumber was not in the list of apartments cases, then the resultant output would be the default "else" condition.

Below is another "else if" example, which uses ranges. Note for each range, upper- or lower-bound values need to have the greater/less than and equal operators:

```
float $x = 12.0;

if ($x > 20.0) {
        print "Larger Case.";
}
else if ($x > 10.0 && $x <= 20.0) {
        print "In Between.";
}
else if ($x > 1.0 && $x <= 10.0) {
        print "Lower Middle.";
}
else {
        print "Lowest.";
}
```

Result: *"In Between."*

There is no limit to the number of tests in an "else if" conditional.

Chapter 4

Character Variables
Strings
Declaring Multiple Data-Types
      String Arrays
Redeclaration of Numerical and Character Data-Types
Concatenation
Concatenation with Variables
Concatenating Numerals
Print Command
Unusual Characters
Replacing and Splitting Long Strings

Character Variables
In general, computers are stupid. They require several lines of code to compute tasks an insect brain can intuitively compute in milliseconds. They must be given the entire sequence of procedures to complete a task, because for the most part, it cannot interpolate or decipher the steps between. They cannot even distinguish between characters and numbers.

This chapter will focus entirely on the topic of characters or groups of characters, also called strings. When first learning computer programming, strings may seem redundant or unimpressive. But mastering alphabetic addition, also called concatenation, will allow a scripter to effectively communicate with the computer through the script editor.

This process is similar to learning a new spoken language. There are often topics lost in translation, words difficult to define, and syntactical complexity. The best practice is to immerse oneself into the scripting process to become fluent with alphabetic and command summation.

Strings
Strings are just sequential characters. The length of the string is dependent upon the quantity of characters in the sequence. Strings can have a length of 0, 1 or a nearly unlimited size. They can be any combination of characters and they must be encapsulated by quotes (" ").

Below are the most common characters which can compose a string:

```
a, b, c, d, e, f, g, h, i, j, k, l, m, n, o, p, q, r,
s, t, u, v, w, x, y, z
A, B, C, D, E, F, G, H, I, J, K, L, M, N, O, P, Q, R,
S, T, U, V, W, X, Y, Z
1, 2, 3, 4, 5, 6, 7, 8, 9, 0
!, @, #, $, %, ^, &, *, (, ), -, _, =, +
[, ], {, }, |, \, ;, :, ', ", ,, ., <, >, /, ?
```

By combining these characters, we can construct words and sentences. Numerals are considered string characters as well, but as long as they are not combined with alphabetic letters, they can be both integers and strings.

```
"Nate"
"12"
"45meters"
"Hello World!"
```

Note spaces are considered characters as well. In the "Hello World!" example, the list consists of *twelve* total keystrokes, with one space, one exclamation point and ten alphabetic characters.

To declare a string, use the term "string."

```
string $SampleStr;
```

The "zero" value for a string appears to be strange. This value is analogous to a float or integer value of 0.
An empty string is shown as ""

```
string $SampleStr1 = "";
```

To declare a string with a non-default initial empty value, assign the value directly:

```
string $SampleStr2 = "Nate";
string $SampleStr3 = "Hello World!";
```

As with integers and floats, strings can be reassigned at any point.

```
string $SampleStr4 = "First Words.";
$SampleStr4 = "Second Words!";
```

```
$SampleStr4 = "Third & Final Words!!";
```

Declaring Multiple Data-Types
String Arrays

Often a scripter will want to store several bits of data simultaneously, but not require the creation of several string variable names. This is common when the count is unknown, large, and/or a combination of the two. These lists of values can be extracted by querying an "index" of the collection.

A user can make a list of floats, integers, or strings. These arrays cannot mix different data-types, so the list must be populated with same types. Declaration of an array appears similar to the singular variables, but with the addition of the bracket characters "[]"

```
string $SampleStrArr[];
```

An unassigned, unset array will have a "size" of zero. Size and assignments are two different concepts: *size* pertains to the number of elements in the list and *assignments* are the values of the elements.

```
string $SampleStrArr2[5];
```

The aforementioned declarations are still unassigned, but have been set. $SampleStrArr2 still has no values stored in it, but it is now limited to a count of six integer elements. All arrays begin with zero, so setting a restriction to the size is always one less than the actual count.

Loading values into an array requires the use of braces "{}." As long as the data-types match, all elements can be delimited by commas.

```
string $SampleStrArr3[] = {"Cat", "Dog", "Fish", "Plant"};
string $SampleStrArr4[] = {"2", "H2", "JP77", "8_!", "&"};
```

In the History Window…

```
// Result: Cat Dog Fish Plant //
// Result: 2 H2 JP77 8_! & //
```

Storing arrays always results in lists separated by spaces. This comes in handy when operating on several objects, which will be discussed in later chapters.

Arrays can also have one element. This is still considered a list, even though the population is a singular value.

```
string $SampleStrArr3[] = {"Singular_Arr_Elem"};
```

To the non-programmer, retrieving elements from an array requires a counter-intuitive sequence. Computers tend to begin with zero, and not one. So counting begins...

0, 1, 2, 3, 4, 5, 6, 7, 8, 9, 10, 11...

For a five element list, the indices would correspond to...

```
//                        0    1    2    3    4
string $SampleStrArr3[] = {"HA!!", "K", "Str", "2*$", "U"};
```

To extract a specific index, the scripter needs only to place the respective whole number in the brackets of the variable name.

```
print $SampleStrArr3[0];
// Result: HA!! //
print $SampleStrArr3[1];
// Result: K //
print $SampleStrArr3[2];
// Result: Str //
print $SampleStrArr3[3];
// Result: 2*$ //
print $SampleStrArr3[4];
// Result: U //
```

A user can break apart an array by extracting values into singular variables. These singular variables must match data-types. If not, integers will truncate the float array values.

```
string $SampleStrArr3[] = {"HA!!", "K", "Str", "2*$", "U"};

string $FirstStr = $SampleStrArr3[0];
// Result: HA!! //
string $SecondStr = $SampleStrArr3[1];
// Result: K //
string $ThirdStr = $SampleStrArr3[2];
// Result: Str //
string $FourthStr = $SampleStrArr3[3];
// Result: 2*$ //
string $FifthStr = $SampleStrArr3[4];
// Result: U //
```

Redeclaration of Numerical and Character Data-Types
Once a variable has been declared and executed, that variable name is stored in the memory with that data-type until the application is closed. There is no way to replace or "redeclare" the data-type from an integer to a string, float to a string, or vector to a string, or vis-versa.

Valid string declaration and assignment:

```
string $Var19 = "2300b";
// Result: 2300b //
```

Incorrect redeclaration from a string to an int:

```
int $Var19 = 2300;
// Error: int $Var19 = 2300; //
// Error: Line 1.12: Invalid redeclaration of variable "$Var19"
as a different type. //
```

Redeclaration is a common error when working collaboratively. Often scripters tend to use the same name for similar variables, however their data-types may differ. The only way to clear the variables is to restart the application or rename it. Renaming is problematic in lengthy codes, because the scripter must find all instances of that name and replace it with the new word.

When working together on a project, separate coders should prefix their variable names with an abbreviation. Then if when the codes are combined, there are no conflicts. In the example below, Veronica and Mike add the characters "V" and "M" before their variables:

```
string $V_Var19 = "2300b";
// Result: 2300b //
int $M_Var19 = 2300;
// Result: 2300 //
```

Concatenation
If mathematics and logic are cornerstones of computational design, then concatenation is another corner. Simply put, concatenation is *alphabetic addition*. Programmers use this technique to build statements, sentences, names, etc.

The operator used to add strings together: +

```
"Hello" + "World!"
```

The result of adding "Hello" to "World!" is…

```
"HelloWorld!"
```

All concatenation is combined by reading from left to right. It will place all of the characters in order.

```
"He" + "ll" + "o " + "Wo" + "rl" + "d!"
```

Result:

```
"Hello World!"
```

Variables can store the concatenated string into a string variable.
String Example 1:

```
string $ConStr1 = "Hello" + "_" + "World!";
// Result: Hello_World! //
```

Concatenating with Variables

Explicit strings are not the only characters that can be concatenated. If variables are added to the sequence, they will be combined as well

The first example adds the two words below.

```
string $Str1 = "Hello";
string $Str2 = "World";

string $ConStr3 = $Str1 + $Str2;
// Result: HelloWorld //
```

However, it should be noted the concatenation was incomplete. Grammar was ignored. The following example would be a more successful concatenation, in terms of readability, with string variables.

```
string $Str1 = "Hello";
string $Str2 = "World";

string $ConStr3 = $Str1 + " " + $Str2 + "!";
// Result: Hello World! //
```

Concatenating Numerals

Numerical variables like integers and floats may also be concatenated into the sequence. When the application detects a possible concatenation outcome, all nested non-string variables are immediately cast as strings, even though the characters are numerals.

```
string $Str1 = "Jane";
string $Str2 = "cats";
int $I2 = 4;

string $ConStr3= $Str1 + " has " + $I2 + " " + $Str2 + ".";
// Result: Jane has 4 cats. //
```

Working with alphabetic addition on numerals can be DANGEROUS. This may appear identical to mathematical addition, but will return counter-intuitive results.

```
Incorrect Concatenation:
int $Val6 = 66;
int $Val7 = 34;
string $ValStr8 = "Total: " + $Val6 + $Val7;
// Result: Total: 6634 //
```

If the intention of the aforementioned example was to add $Val6 to $Val7 mathematically, then it has clearly not functioned properly. Instead of returning a string with the addition of 66 + 34 = 100, the application has calculated the incorrect summation to be 66 + 34 = 6,634. As stated before, once the application detects any string concatenation, then all of the nested non-string variables are cast as strings. $Val6 and $Val7 are now each stored as the two characters ("66" and "34") and not their actual numerical values; to the computer "66" + "34" is actually "6634".

The best way to calculate mathematical addition while concatenating is to dedicate a variable for the arithmetic sequences or to surround any initial calculation with parentheses.

Dedicating a variable:
```
int $Val6 = 66;
int $Val7 = 34;
int $DedVal = $Val6 + $Val7;
string $ValStr8 = "Total: " + $DedVal;
// Result: Total: 100 //
```

Using parentheses to prioritize calculations:
```
int $Val6 = 66;
int $Val7 = 34;
string $ValStr8 = "Total: " + ($Val6 + $Val7);
// Result: Total: 100 //
```

Print Command
For some of the previous chapters, this textbook has been using a command called "print." The next chapter will discuss commands more in depth, but "print" is an exception. This command is the simplest method in the programming interface. Not to be confused with File > Print in the application user-interface, "print" is a command which, in its nicest form, states the value of a variable.

The syntax for "print" is as follows:
[The Name of the Command] [The String(s)]

```
print "Hello World.";
```

Result: *"Hello World."*

When working with single or non-concatenated string sequence, the command requires only a space to separate it from the printed value.
Single String Print Example:

```
string $SStr2 = "Testing Print.";
print $SStr2;
```

Result: *"Testing Print."*

However, when printing a concatenated sequence, the variables must be surrounded by parentheses, or errors will result.

Incorrect use of "print," with missing parentheses:

```
string $SStr2 = "Testing";
string $SStr3 = "Print";
print $SStr2 + " " + $SStr3 + ".";
// Error: print $SStr2 + " " + $SStr3 + "."; //
// Error: Line 3.14: Syntax error //
```

Proper syntax with "print," by prioritizing the concatenation first:

```
string $SStr2 = "Testing";
string $SStr3 = "Print";
print ($SStr2 + " " + $SStr3 + ".");
```

Result: *"Testing Print."*

Unusual Characters
The character map is not limited to standard ascii keys. The developers have exposed non-standard keys for scenarios not typically typed into a string. This is accomplished by preceding the desired content with the backslash ("\") key. This allows scripters to place the equivalent of the "Tab," "Enter," and "Quotation Mark" keys into their strings.

All specialized keys are two-character combinations:

Tab: "\t"
Enter: "\n"
Quote: "\""

Return Example 1:

```
print ("Nate\nSteve\nReturn Test");
```

Result: *"Nate*
             Steve
             Return Test"

Return Example 2:

```
string $J1 = "Nate";
string $J2 = "Steve";
string $J3 = "Return Test";

print ($J1 + "\n" + $J2 + "\n" + $J3);
```

Result: *"Nate*
           Steve
           Return Test"

Replacing and Splitting Long Strings

Unlike the previous examples, strings can be very long, sometimes having more than thousands of characters at any given moment. There will be occurrences where portions of the string will need to be split or broken down into manageable portions. These portions will be stored in the memory as elements in a large string array, and each index is determined by a divisor character or characters.

Splitting strings into arrays takes some preparation. First, there must be initial declarations; $MainArr4 is an empty string array, which will remain empty until a later time. $MainStr4 is the large string to be divided.

```
string $MainArr4[];
string $MainStr4 = "A_B_C_D_E_F_G_H_I_J_K";
```

The last line conducts the splitting and also counts the number of new portions. The command utilized is called "tokenize" and it requires three inputs: 1.) The string to be split, 2.) the divider character(s), 3.) and the empty string array to place the portions.

```
int $MainArr4Count = tokenize($MainStr4, "_", $MainArr4);
```

In this example, the divider is just the character "_". As the application processes the large string, it cuts the characters in-between and appends them to the output array. This becomes a new index and will continue until the string has ended.

All together...

```
string $MainArr4[];
string $MainStr4 = "A_B_C_D_E_F_G_H_I_J_K";
int $MainArr4Count = tokenize($MainStr4, "_", $MainArr4);
// Result: 11 //
```

Result: *"A*
           B
           C
           D
           ...
           K"

The History Window may only display the count (// Result: 11 //), this is deceiving. Behind the scenes, the $MainArr4 has been loaded with eleven separate character string indices. If unsure, the scripter can always print the contents of the array.

String Splitting Example 2:

```
string $MainArr5[];
string $MainStr5 = "abracadabra abacus";
int $MainArr5Count = tokenize($MainStr5, "ab", $MainArr5);
// Result: 6 //
print $MainArr5;
```

Result: *"r*
            c
            d
            r

            cus"

The divider characters ("ab") are not sequential. This will split the words at any occurrence of the characters.

Constructing clear strings will be a major component for later chapters.

Chapter 5

Commands
Format and Flags
Help
Concatenation and Parentheses in Commands
Edit and Query Flags (Backticks)

Commands
Up until this chapter, the focus of this textbook has been on passive capacities of computer programming, like storing and testing information. This and subsequent chapters will be dealing with more active functionalities of scripting. The most prevalent tools are called commands, or methods.

Commands are procedures that accomplish tasks. Some commands return and create data and others just generate content. Since the goal of this manual is to work three- or four-dimensionally, most of this chapter will focus on basic geometric functions.

Format and Flags
Commands have a loose, but standard structure. The command name always appears first. Second, input values preceded by "flags" pepper the interior, and lastly, geometric inputs follow the sequence. Some commands may have no flags or inputs, and any ignored value has a typically-zero default. Others may have dozens of input flags and values.

"print" is a simple command with only one input (a string) and no flags.

```
print "Hello World!";
```

"sphere" has eleven flags:

```
sphere -p 0 0 0 -ax 0 1 0 -ssw 0 -esw 360 -r 1 -d 3 -ut 0 -tol
0.01 -s 12 -nsp 12 -ch 1;
```

Help
All flags begin with a dash character and are followed by either a full or abbreviated name. Each flag stands for a required input for a particular command. When utilizing a new command, a scripter can list all possible flags by invoking the "help" command. "help" will print off all of the pertinent information into the History Window and give both the long and abbreviated flag strings, along with their respective required inputs. The command reference has the same input information, along with more detailed descriptions.

To run the "help" method, in the Input Window, type…

```
help sphere;
```

The History Window prints the following:

```
// Result:
Synopsis: sphere [flags] [String...]
Flags:
    -e -edit
    -q -query
   -ax -axis                    Length Length Length
  -cch -caching                 on|off
   -ch -constructionHistory     on|off
    -d -degree                  Int
  -esw -endSweep                Angle
   -hr -heightRatio             Float
    -n -name                    String
  -nds -nodeState               Int
  -nsp -spans                   Int
    -o -object                  on|off
    -p -pivot                   Length Length Length
   -po -polygon                 Int
    -r -radius                  Length
    -s -sections                Int
  -ssw -startSweep              Angle
  -tol -tolerance               Length
   -ut -useTolerance            on|off
//
```

Upon review, the chart generated by the "help" command for "sphere" contains nineteen possible flags, with corresponding inputs of data-types ranging from strings, integers, floats, and float arrays. The first column lists the abbreviated, or short, flag names. These shortened names are the most widely-used variant of the command syntax.

```
sphere -r 0.5;
```

The second column lists the long flag name. While long flags may require extra seconds to type, coding is more didactic and less prone to error. It is common to find different commands with identical (but definitively distinct) short flags.

```
sphere -radius 0.5;
```

The last column in the help chart pertains to the type of desired variable input relating to the flag. In the case of the command "sphere," the flag "radius" corresponds to something called a "length." All measurable types can be replaced with a float or integer. Values set up with "string" or "on|off" require only character information. For the flag "-radius" necessitates a "Length" value; coders should place a float or float variable.

```
sphere -r 0.5;
```

or...

```
float $RadVal = 0.5;
sphere -r $RadVal;
```

Concatenation and Parentheses in Commands

When commands generate new things (i.e. geometry, objects, etc), it is best practice to name the outputs. Also, it is common to complete mathematical calculations in the command syntax. Both of these issues require the use of parentheses to set the priority of the tasks. If no parentheses are found, errors result.

When a scripter wants to complete a calculation inside of a command, the formula must be encapsulated within parentheses. For example, if a variable ($RadVal) has been assigned to a float, and the desired radius is two-times the variable, users can complete the multiplication process in the command.
Incorrect float calculation:

```
float $RadVal = 0.25;
sphere -r 2 * $RadVal;
// Error: sphere -r 2 * $RadVal; //
// Error: Line 2.13: Syntax error //
```

Correct float calculation:

```
float $RadVal = 0.25;
sphere -r (2 * $RadVal);
```

As with numerical calculations, string concatenation must be prioritized. This is typical when coders want to build unique names for newly created objects.
Incorrect string concatenation:

```
string $CircName = "Em";
int $CircCount = 3;
sphere -r 0.5 -n $CircName + $CircCount;
// Error: sphere -r 0.5 -n $CircName + $CircCount; //
// Error: Line 3.28: Syntax error //
```

Correct string concatenation:

```
string $CircName = "Em";
int $CircCount = 3;
sphere -r 0.5 -n ($CircName + $CircCount);
```

Edit and Query Flags (Backticks)

Every command will create something. However, some commands have dual or triple uses to retrieve or set new information on existing objects. This is called "querying" and "editing," respectively. When developing dynamic systems, regardless if scripted or manually constructed, recovering localized data is extremely important. Once stored, this information can be reinfused into the system by editing its current state.

The syntax for editing is nearly identical to creating, with the first flag being "-e" and the last string identifying the existing object. Once the application reads the "-e" flag, all following flags will be modified. Note, a user cannot have create and edit flags simultaneously.

Single Value Edit Flag Example 1:

```
sphere -r 0.6 -n "SphereObj22";
sphere -e -r 2.25 SphereObj22;
```

Result: *"SphereObj22" will have its radius increased to 2.25 units.*

Multi-Value Edit Flag Example 2:

```
sphere -p 0 0 0 -n "SphereObj22";
sphere -e -p 2 -2 4 SphereObj22;
```

Result: *"SphereObj22" moved from the origin to (2, -2, 4).*

Querying geometry and objects requires a more radical syntax change. This process entails the declaration of a variable to store the queried data, the use of backtick characters and the addition of the "-q" flag.

The variable data-type must correspond to the command's input flag type, as described in the command or help reference. Flags requiring "Length," "Angle," or other real number values will need the declaration of a float or integer. Flags that mention three or more values require an array data-type, and flags needing characters like "off," "on," or names will necessitate a string.

Backticks (`), also known as grave accents, are underused characters found to the left of the number "1" key that share a resemblance to shifted apostrophes. This character acts like parentheses when surrounding commands; they force the application to complete the innermost processes first and report the data for querying. It is imperative programmers use backticks (`) and not apostrophes ('), for mixing these characters will result in an error. With the exception of forgetting the end semicolon, misusing backticks is probably the second most common error in MEL scripting. Since the backtick is minimally utilized outside the programming world, web-posted and emailed MEL scripts occasionally replace backtick characters with apostrophes.

To finalize the queried sequence, precede the requested flag with "-q" and end the list with the name of the existing object.

Single Value Querying Example 1:

```
sphere -r 0.6 -n "SphereObj22";
float $RadVal = `sphere -q -r SphereObj22`;
// Result: 0.6 //
```

Result: *Float "$RadVal" has a value of 0.6*

Multi Value Querying Example 1:

```
sphere -p 0 -2.1 0 -n "SphereObj22";
float $SphPos[] = `sphere -q -p SphereObj22`;
// Result: 0 -2.1 0 //
```

Result: *Float array "$SphPos" now has three elements: 0, 2.1, and 0*

Chapter 6

Basic Geometry
NURBS, Polygons, Subdivision Surfaces
NURBS Primitives
      "sphere"
      "nurbsPlane"
      "nurbsCube"
      "cylinder"
      "cone"
      "torus"
Polygon Primitives
      "polySphere"
      "polyPlane"
      "polyCube"
      "polyCylinder"
      "polyCone"
      "polyTorus"
Nonstandard Flags
Redundant History Window Outputs
Subdivision Surface Primitives

Basic Geometry
All three-dimensional modeling applications have a catalog of objects called primitives. These shapes can usually be found in a child's wooden block set and are good places to begin one's exposure to form. Depending on the make-up of a particular primitive, these objects can be combined to aggregate any type of output collection.

The same primitive shapes can have differing compositions, each exhibiting diverse behaviors. If one could extend the definition of the word "construction" to virtual objects, primitives are constructed of a combination of singular- and poly-surface conditions. Also, there exist three types of geometry surfacing techniques, somewhat comparable to physical textures. Each texture will produce an alternative smoothing variation, which up to the designer's aesthetic decisions, will impact the overall look of the project. With experience, users will grow accustomed to the variations of these forms and assign the appropriate shapes accordingly.

NURBS, Polygons, Subdivision Surfaces
The application has provided three types of surface constructions: NURBS surfaces, polygons, and subdivision surfaces. Each type affords the designer alternative texturing possibilities.

NURBS (Non-uniform Rational B-Spline) surfaces are smooth, mathematically-driven constructions that are manipulated by altering the location and tension of control vertices (C.V.'s). These vertices are laid out on a "grid" on the surface, where U is reserved for the CV count in one direction and V is set aside to describe the counter direction. NURBS surfaces are simlar to longitude and latitude lines on a globe or map. For open NURBS surfaces, the U and V coordinate system forms a grid on the surface, much like Mercator Projection mapping. For closed surfaces like a sphere, the U's and V's can best described as latitude and longitude lines on a globe. These control lines are nicknamed "isoparms" or "isoparm curves." For scripting with NURBS geometry, the grid system will be a simple means of navigating the surface.

Polygons are faceted three-dimensional shapes, sometimes called meshes. Facets fall into two categories: triangles and quadrilaterals. All triangles, by their nature, are planar, but quads can be planar or comprised of two adjacent triangles. All faces on a polygon are controlled by control and face vertices, however unlike NURBS geometry, there exists no smoothing of these values. A good example of a polygonalized sphere is a disco ball. From a distance, the disco ball appears to be a smooth sphere, but upon closer inspection, the mirrored object has several hundred flat faces.

Subdivision surfaces are smoothed polygonalized geometry. Often called "Sub-D's," these constructions are didactically named; the angles between faces are recursively "subdivided" until the illusion of smoothing occurs. Subdivision surfaces are exceptionally malleable geometric objects and require no rigid U and V framework, thus they can be molded into any imaginable form. They analog equivalent to Sub-D's would be soft clay; the blob can be bent, compressed, ripped and healed into any topology.

NURBS Primitives
NURBS are the building blocks for 3D design. Therefore, they are the best place to begin. The set of NURBS primitives are as follows: sphere, cube, cylinder, cone, plane and torus.

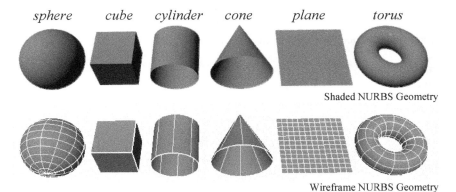

 sphere *cube* *cylinder* *cone* *plane* *torus*

Shaded NURBS Geometry

Wireframe NURBS Geometry

"sphere"
To create a default sphere:

```
sphere;
```

Result: *A default sphere named "nurbsSphere1" is created.*

A default size sphere has a radius of 1, location at the origin (0, 0, 0) and a name beginning with the prefix "nurbsSphere." If there exists other default name spheres in this session, the application will append the name string of "nurbsSphere" with n+1 of smallest number suffix, where "n" is the last number. I.E., if the last sphere in the file is named "nurbsSphere45," then this newly-created sphere would be named "nurbsSphere46." This naming convention is repeated for any duplicate existing strings, because the application must have unique naming

The default settings for the "sphere" command are limiting and utilization of flags will expand a scripters capabilities. Important flags for "sphere" are *pivot*, *radius*, *axis* and *name*. *Pivot* requires an XYZ coordinate of floats and sets the position of the sphere. The *Axis* pertains to the orientation of the object, which also needs a three-element float array. *Radius* and *Name* use common definitions.

```
-p      or      -pivot
-r      or      -radius
-ax     or      -axis
-n      or      -name
```

```
sphere -p 0 1 -2 -r 0.75 -ax 0 0.5 0.7 -n "Sph1";
```

Result: *A tilted axis sphere named "Sph1" appears at (0, 1, -2) with a radius of
¾.*

Several other flags give access to other characteristics of the sphere. The
aforementioned flags are most commonly used, and the manual will only
describe the main flags. Coders should research all of the geometry commands
from the reference for more nuanced exposure.

"nurbsPlane"
To create a default NURBS plane:

```
nurbsPlane;
```

Result: *A default plane object named "nurbsPlane1" is created.*

Planes are infinitely thin flat surfaces. Flags of significance are *width, length
ratio, pivot,* and *U* and *V* isoparm counts. While the width is inputed outright,
the length of the rectangle is relatively determined as a ratio of the width. The
default setting for the isoparm coordinates are 1 and 1 (straight), however
utilizing flags "–u" and "–v" will increase the surface NURBS resolution.

```
-p      or      -pivot
-w      or      -width
-lr     or      -lengthRatio
-u      or      -patchesU
-v      or      -patchesV
-n      or      -name
```

```
nurbsPlane -p 0 0 20 -w 2 -lr 1.5 -u 12 -v 12 -n "NPL5";
```

Result: *A 2x3, 12-isoparm plane named "NPL5" is offset from the XY plane at
20 units.*

"nurbsCube"
To create a default NURBS cube:

```
nurbsCube;
```

Result: *A default cube named "nurbsCube1" is created.*

Since NURBS geometry consists of a structured grid, it is impossible to produce
a closed six-sided rectilinear prism out of just one NURBS surface. The
application resolves this by grouping six nurbsPlanes in the formation of a cube.
Each face has a unique name ("topnurbsCube1," "bottomnurbsCube1,"
"leftnurbsCube1,"   "rightnurbsCube1,"   "frontnurbsCube1,"   and
"backnurbsCube1") and the group is given the cube name ("nurbsCube1").

Similar to nurbsPlane flags, *pivot, axis, width, length ratio, height ratio,* and *name* are most pertinent for cubes.   Like nurbsPlane lengthRatio inputs, heightRatio flags require the determination of the width value. Axis flags force the orientation of the cube.

```
-p      or      -pivot
-w      or      -width
-lr     or      -lengthRatio
-hr     or      -heightRatio
-a      or      -axis
-n      or      -name
```

```
nurbsCube -p -1 9 0 -ax 0 .5 0.7 -w 2 -lr 1.5 -hr 2 -n "NC6";
```

Result: *A tilted 2x3x4 cube named "NC6" is placed at (-1, 9, 0).*

"cylinder"
To create a default NURBS cylinder:

```
cylinder;
```

Result: *A default cylinder named "nurbsCylinder1" is created.*

Cylinders consist of a revolved plane which closes in one isoparm direction. Two geometric flags of relevance are *radius* and *heightRatio,* and *sections* divides the surface into an input integer of isoparm divisions.

```
-p      or      -pivot
-r      or      -radius
-hr     or      -heightRatio
-s      or      -sections
-a      or      -axis
-n      or      -name
```

```
cylinder -p 0 10 0 -ax 0 -0.5 0.3 -r 3.5 -hr 2 -s 8 -n "NCYL8";
```

Result: *A tilted cylinder of radius 3.5, height 7 and isoparm count 8 is created at (0, 10, 0).*

"cone"
To create a default NURBS cone:

```
cone;
```

Result: *A default cone named "nurbsCone1" is created.*

The "Cone" command is nearly identical to cylinder. Still consisting of a revolution, this has one counter-directional isoparm where the control vertices all meet at one point in space. This is the point of the cone.

```
-p    or    -pivot
-r    or    -radius
-hr   or    -heightRatio
-s    or    -sections
-a    or    -axis
-n    or    -name
```

```
cone -p 0.1 0 -10 -ax 0 0.1 0.9 -r 3.5 -hr 2 -s 8 -n "NN3";
```

Result: *A tilted cone of radius 3.5, height 7 and isoparm count 8 is created at (0.1, 0, -10).*

"torus"
To create a default NURBS torus:

```
torus;
```

Result: *A default torus named "nurbsTorus1" is created.*

The last in the series of revolved shapes, the torus resembles a doughnut form. This shape is unique because unlike all of the other NURBS primitives, the torus has a hole. When setting the revolved radius, use the "-r" flag, but determining the profile radius, use the "-hr" flag. It is imperative scripters always maintain a heightRatio of equal or lesser value to the torus' revolved radius. Height ratios of greater values will create a self-intersecting torus, devoid of a hole.

```
torus -p 20 0 0 -ax 0.2 0 1 -r 2 -hr 0.5 -s 8 -n "NT2";
```

Result: *A tilted torus of radius 2 and profile radius 1 is created at (20, 0, 0).*

Polygon Primitives

As previously stated, polygons are faceted meshes. Zoomed out, poly primitives are very similar to the NURBS base shapes, except NURBS forms are generally open. Excluding the polyPlane, all polygon primitives are "closed," completely capable of encapsulating a volume of space. The polyCube, unlike its grouped NURBS equivalent, is a singular closed object.

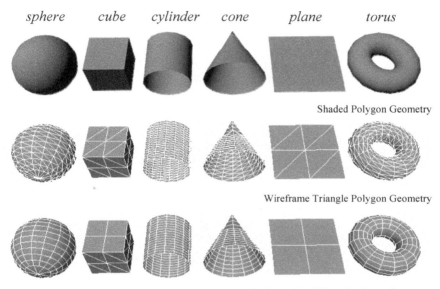

sphere   cube   cylinder   cone   plane   torus

Shaded Polygon Geometry

Wireframe Triangle Polygon Geometry

Wireframe Quadrilateral Polygon Geometry

"polySphere"

To create a default polygonalized sphere:

```
polySphere;
```

Result: *A default polygonalized sphere named "pSphere1" is created.*

A default size sphere has a radius of 1, location at the origin (0, 0, 0) and a name beginning with the prefix "pSphere." If there exist other default name spheres in this session, the application will append the name string of "pSphere" with the next unused number. This naming convention is repeated for any duplicate existing strings because the application must have unique naming.

Important flags for "sphere" are *radius, axis, subdivisionsX, subdivisionsY,* and *name.* It should be noted, poly primitives have no pivot flag to determine the location of the object. This places all objects at the origin. The *Axis* pertains to the orientation of the object, which also needs a three-element float array. If the scripter desires to increase the vertex count of the sphere, modify the *subdivisionsX* and *subdivisionsY* integers. These values are relatively similar to "sections" for NURBS primitive flags, but replace the characters "U" and "V". *Radius* and *Name* use common definitions.

```
-r    or    -radius
-ax   or    -axis
-sx   or    -subdivisionsX
-sy   or    -subdivisionsY
-n    or    -name
```

```
polySphere -r 1.75 -sx 12 -sy 11 -ax 0 1 0.5 -n "PLYSPH1";
```

Result: *A tilted axis polygonalized sphere named "PLYSPH1" with a radius of 1¾ is created. It has a faceted grid of 11 x 12 vertices.*

"polyPlane"
To create a default polygonalized plane:

```
polySphere;
```

Result: *A default polygonalized plane named "pPlane1" is created.*

Unlike the difficulty with height and length ratios in NURBS primitives, polygonalized shapes require only direct *width* and *height* floats. *Axis, subdivisionsX, subdivisionsY,* and *name* are the same for all poly primitives.

```
-w    or    -width
-h    or    -height
-ax   or    -axis
-sx   or    -subdivisionsX
-sy   or    -subdivisionsY
-n    or    -name
```

```
polyPlane -w 1.2 -h 3.5 -sx 5 -sy 5 -ax 0 0.2 1 -n "PPL5";
```

Result: *A tilted axis 1.2 x 3.5 polygonalized plane named "PPL5" is created. It has a faceted grid of 5 x 5 vertices.*

"polyCube"
To create a default polygonalized cube:

```
polyCube;
```

Result: *A default polygonalized cube named "pCube1" is created.*

polyCubes can be thought of as polyPlanes with a third dimension of functionality. In addition to the *width, height, axis, subdivisionsX, subdivisionsY,* and *name* flags, *depth* and *subdivisionsZ* complete the attribute list. These dimensions do not correspond to the coordinate system of the file, but rather the suffixes "X,"

"Y," and "Z" are just a means of categorizing the directionality of the subdivision of the mesh.

```
-w    or    -width
-h    or    -height
-d    or    -depth
-ax   or    -axis
-sx   or    -subdivisionsX
-sy   or    -subdivisionsY
-sz   or    -subdivisionsZ
-n    or    -name
```

```
polyCube -w 4 -h 3 -d 2 -sx 3 -sy 4 -sz 5 -ax 0 1 0.2 -n "PC3";
```

Result: *A closed, tilted axis 4x3x2 polygonalized cube named "PC3" is created. It has a faceted matrix of 3x4x5 vertices, respectively.*

"polyCylinder"
To create a default polygonalized cylinder:

```
polyCylinder;
```

Result: *A default polygonalized cylinder named "pCylinder1" is created.*

PolyCylinders are closed meshes in the shape of a facet cylinder. Flags of significance are the *radius, height, subdivisionsX, subdivisionsY, subdivisionsZ, axis,* and *name*. SubdivisionZ for polyCylinders and polyCones has a unique characteristic where the dividing occurs radially from the centroid of the flat faces, as opposed to other three-dimensional polygon geometry. When assigning the Z divisions, the value of one (1) places "spokes" of mesh edges concentrically; the value of zero (0) reduces the face count to just one, with no divisions.

```
-r    or    -radius
-h    or    -height
-ax   or    -axis
-sx   or    -subdivisionsX
-sy   or    -subdivisionsY
-sz   or    -subdivisionsZ
-n    or    -name
```

```
polyCylinder -r 2.4 -h 2.8 -sx 20 -sy 10 -sz 5 -ax 0 0.6 0.2 -n "PCY3";
```

Result: *A tilted axis 2.4 radius x 2.8 high polygonalized cylinder named "PCY3" is created. It has a faceted matrix of 20x10x5 vertices arranged radially from the principal axis.*

"polyCone"
To create a default polygonalized cone:

```
polyCone;
```

Result: *A default polygonalized cone named "pCone1" is created.*

Cones and Cylinders share nearly all of the same functionality.

```
-r     or     -radius
-h     or     -height
-ax    or     -axis
-sx    or     -subdivisionsX
-sy    or     -subdivisionsY
-sz    or     -subdivisionsZ
-n     or     -name
```

```
polyCone -r 1.4 -h 2.8 -sx 20 -sy 10 -sz 3 -ax 0 1 0.5 -n "PCNE7";
```

Result: *A tilted axis 1.4 radius x 2.8 high polygonalized cone named "PCNE7" is created. It has a faceted matrix of 20x10x3 vertices arranged radially from the principal axis.*

"polyTorus"
To create a default polygonalized torus:

```
polyTorus;
```

Result: *A default polygonalized torus named "pTorus1" is created.*

Because the torus has no hard edges like the polyCube, polyCylinder and polyCube, the dimensions of sectioning are restricted to two direction, *subdivisionsX* and *subdivisionsY*. *Radius*, *sectionRadius*, and *twist* are torus-specific attributes which identify the main axis radius, the profile radius, and twist along the profile. *Axis* and *name* complete this unique flag list.

```
-r     or     -radius
-sr    or     -sectionRadius
-tw    or     -twist
-ax    or     -axis
-sx    or     -subdivisionsX
-sy    or     -subdivisionsY
-n     or     -name
```

```
polyTorus -r 2.3 -sr 1.2 -tw 10 -sx 8 -sy 6 -ax 0 1 0.3 -n "PT77";
```

Result: *A tilted axis 2.3x1.2 polygonalized torus with a 10 degree twist named "PT77" is created.*

Nonstandard Flags
As with all commands, some flags are used more frequently than others. This chapter, while displaying all of the primitive commands, only showcased typical flags for brevity. With greater familiarity of the scripting language, users should expand their repertoire for more nuanced flags. These can be found in the command reference. For example, the "sphere" method has several more flags than just radius, axis, pivot, and name. Caching, construction history, degrees of curvature, end- and start-sweeps, height, nodeState, spans, polygons, sections, tolerances, and the ability to set tolerances also populate the flag list for "sphere," totaling nineteen dedicated attributes. New releases of the application introduce enhancements to the language like more commands and longer flag lists; constant re-education and investigation of MEL is prudent.

Redundant History Window Outputs:
When recording basic geometry commands, a scripter will notice extra history lines. In most cases, these lines are useless and can be removed if brought into the Input Window. For example, the torus icon button was manually pressed by a user, and the History Window prints...

```
CreateNURBSTorus;
torus -p 0 0 0 -ax 0 0 1 -ssw 0 -esw 360 -msw 360 -r 1 -hr 0.5
-d 3 -ut 0 -tol 0.01 -s 8 -nsp 4 -ch 1; objectMoveCommand;
```

The function "CreateNURBSTorus" is the installed one-line MEL script that executes the single line code below it. Any command line with the word "Create" as a prefix is a strong indicator the button has a dedicated MEL file associated to it. The command is irrelevant for coding purposes. It is poor practice to use these functions; only utilize the core geometry commands like "sphere," "polyCube," nurbsCube, et cetera. Also, avoid placing the "objectMoveCommand" in the script. This will not positively or negatively impact the result of the code.

Lastly, the use of the "Create" functions will often generate abnormal results. The most common consequence is the doubling of the scene's geometric population. Also, "Create" functions also return no name string data, leaving the scene with doubled, default objects.

Subdivision Surface Primitives
Subdivision surfaces are smoothed meshes, but not primitives as conventionally understood with polygons or NURBS. It is a common misconception that sub-d primitives are unique geometric entities in Maya, however this is an illusion. In actuality, the functions generating subdivision surfaces are simple MEL scripts converting polygon primitives. This is based on the method "polyToSubdiv" which will convert any open or closed mesh into a smoothed sub-d surface. This book will address conversion commands like "polyToSubdiv" in later chapters.

Knowing subdivision surfaces are not dedicated forms, their accessibility is limited and difficult to traverse. Polygons and NURBS geometry have a well-established infrastructure, while sub-d's require unusual circuitous methods of creation, naming, modification and removal.

It is poor practice to use "Create" functions to generate standard forms, but for beginner scripters, these tools are adequate for subdivisions. Later chapters will explain better ways of making this type of geometry.

```
CreateSubdivSphere;
CreateSubdivCube;
CreateSubdivCylinder;
CreateSubdivCone;
CreateSubdivPlane;
CreateSubdivTorus;
```

Result: *Objects created: "subdivSphere1" "subdivCube1" "subdivCylinder1" "subdivCone1" "subdivPlane1" and "subdivTorus1"*

Using "Create" commands forces the scripter with only two ways to obtain the resultant geometry: naming conventions and selection. One can expect the following when parsing the contents of a newly created sub-d object:

"subdiv" + shape type + number

Also, with all creation commands, the last object generated is selected. This is important for the next chapter, because a selected object can undergo transformations.

Chapter 7

Basic Transformation
Selection
      "select"
Translation
      "move"
      World Space Translation
      Relative Translation
Rotation
      "rotate"
      Absolute Rotation
      Relative Rotation
      Pivot Position
Scale
      "scale"
      Absolute Scaling
      Relative Scaling
      Pivot Position
Xform Matrix
Difference between Flag Position and Transform Position
Duplication

Basic Transformation
All three-dimensional modeling applications have basic transformation techniques. Transformation procedures are commands which operate on existing geometry by global modification, but contrary to last chapter's topics, do not actually create any objects. When thinking of children's building blocks, primitives are shapes and transformation commands are actions. These procedures move and orient the blocks from the storage container into aggregations.

The three most prevalent cross-platform procedures are translating, rotating and scaling. Translation, or "move," takes an object and places it in a new location. Rotation, or "rotate," configures the orientation of the object based on a pivot location. Scaling, or "scale," proportionally resizes the object based on a pivot location. These commands can be manipulated relative to the object's current position or to a world space location or orientation. Other cross-platform commands are selection and duplication, which are equally essential procedures for three-dimensional modeling.

Selection
All procedures available in the user interface are exposed to the scripting language. The act of selection also follows this axiom. When a user wishes to move/rotate/scale an object, they must first select the object by clicking on it. This highlights the object until an operation has occurred, or if the user deselects or replaces the selection.

There are several types of selection, all determined by flag configurations. In the following examples, three spheres have been added to the scene to showcase the different selection types. This code should be run prior to testing future "select," "move," "rotate," and "scale" examples.

```
sphere -r 0.5 -p 1 2 2;
sphere -r 0.75 -p -1 -2 -2;
sphere -r 1 -p 1 -2 2;
```

Result: *nurbsSphere1, nurbsSphere2, nurbsSphere3.*

"select"
To select a previously created object ("nurbsSphere1"):

```
select nurbsSphere1;
```

Result: *A previously created object named "nurbsSphere1" was selected.*

Flagless selections are not a best practice. When possible, scripters should use the standard selection flags to filter geometry. Names and/or arrays of names will follow the input flags like *replace*, *toggle*, and *deselect*, while *clear* requires no additional information.

```
-cl     or      -clear
-d      or      -deselect
-r      or      -replace
-tgl    or      -toggle
```

Before instruction on the selection of objects begins, users should understand deselection. Because selections can be additive, not starting with a clean slate will impact the results of future commands.
To clear the selection…

```
select -cl;
```

Result: *Any selected objects are cleared from the selection set.*

The replacement flag tends to be the typical mode for selection. In one step, this flag substitutes the current selection with the input name. These substitutions can occur with a singular object name, a list of sequential names, or an array of names. When considering pluralities of strings, the selection count can be

unlimited. Note: if the previous selection is empty, replacement will simply add the named components to the selection.
To replace the current selection...

```
select -r nurbsSphere1;
```

Result: *The object "nurbsSphere1" replaces the current selection (if any).*

To replace the current selection with a list of names...

```
select -r nurbsSphere1 nurbsSphere2;
```

Result: *The objects "nurbsSphere1" and "nurbSphere2" replace the current selection (if any).*

To replace the current selection with an array of name strings...

```
string $Names[] = {"nurbsSphere1", "nurbsSphere2"};
select -r $Names;
```

Result: *The objects "nurbsSphere1" and "nurbSphere2" replace the current selection (if any).*

The use of the asterisks character, commonly called the "wildcard," allows the selection of all objects sharing partial name strings. For example, the strings "nick" and "nicole" begin with the letters "nic". Utilizing the wildcard, the string "nic*" searches for all names sharing these letters, followed by any string combination. The word "janice" also has the characters "nic" in it, but these sub-letters do not preface the name. In this case, two asterisks would be necessary to prompt all three strings, "*nic*", to query all strings that may have (or have no) characters preceding and/or succeeding it.
To replace the current selection with any objects beginning with the letters "nurbsSphere"...

```
select -r "nurbsSphere*";
```

Result: *The objects "nurbsSphere1," "nurbSphere2," and "nurbsSphere3" replace the current selection (if any).*

Objects are either selected or not selected; something cannot be half or 3/8ths selected. This characteristic of selection permits a user to use a process called "toggling." If the object is selected, toggling will deselect it. If the object is not selected, toggling will select it. Also, toggling is an additive (or reductive) process; the current selection will not be replaced.
To replace the current selection and add another object to the selection...

```
select -r nurbsSphere3;
select -tgl nurbsSphere1;
```

Result: *The object "nurbsSphere3" replace the current selection and "nurbsSphere1" is added to the new selection.   Note: the first replacement clears the previous selection, so it is known that "nurbsSphere1" is not highlighted.*

To select the same object twice…

```
select -r nurbsSphere1;
select -tgl nurbsSphere1;
```

Result: *Nothing is selected.*

To use toggle for a sequence…

```
select -r nurbsSphere3;
select -tgl nurbsSphere1;
select -tgl nurbsSphere2;
```

Result: *The objects "nurbsSphere3," "nurbSphere1," and "nurbsSphere2" replace the current selection (if any), in that order.*

Translation

Movement deals with the alteration of an object's X, Y and Z location. The object is currently located at Point A (X_1, Y_1, Z_1), and the move command requests a new destination coordinate Point B (X_2, Y_2, Z_2). The limits to translating an object can be from nearly negative infinity to positive infinity, and the stasis condition for moving is zero.

"move"

To default move an object:

```
move 2 2 2;
```

Result: *The previously selected object(s) was moved to the coordinate (2, 2, 2).*

Moving objects is accomplished with two distinct and significant flags: *relative* and *world space*.   These flags should never occur in the same line simultaneously. By default, this method will translate the currently selected object; if this previously-selected object is not to be translated, a user can force the targeted object directly by calling for it. The "move" command can be paired with a select line or the name of the object can follow the position coordinates. Also, like the select command, this can operate on singular names, name lists and name arrays.

```
-r     or     -relative
-ws    or     -worldSpace
```

World Space Translation

World space calculations prove beneficial when scripters need an object to shift to a predetermined location.

To select an object and move it to a position in space...

```
select -r nurbsSphere1;
move -ws 2.0 -2.1 4.2;
```

Result: *"nurbsSphere1" has been moved from its current position to the coordinate (2.0, -2.1, 4.2).*

To move an object to a position in space...

```
move -ws 2.0 -2.1 4.2 nurbsSphere1;
```

Result: *"nurbsSphere1" has been moved from its current position to the coordinate (2.0, -2.1, 4.2). Note: "nurbsSphere1" did not need to be selected.*

Relative Translation

Relative translations are useful when scripters are working more dynamically. The application will take the object and move it based on its current location.

To select an object and move relative to its current location...

```
select -r nurbsSphere1;
move -r 1.9 -1.5 3.2;
```

Result: *"nurbsSphere1" has been moved from its current position exactly (1.9, -1.5, 3.2) units.*

To move an object relative to its current location...

```
move -r 1.9 -1.5 3.2 nurbsSphere1;
```

Result: *"nurbsSphere1" has been moved from its current position exactly (1.9, -1.5, 3.2) units. Note: "nurbsSphere1" did not need to be selected.*

Rotation

When users wish to modify an objects orientation, rotation is the preferred method. Rotations require three float values in degree units, corresponding to the local XYZ axis system. Unlike the move command, the pivot location of the object is extremely important, because this establishes the anchor for rotational transformation. The orientation per axis can be summed as a "right-hand rule," where the thumb correlates to the axis direction and fingers imply the angular rotation (in degrees). In mathematical circles, these revolutions are called Euler angles.

Mathematically, a scripter would only need to work from 0 to 360 degrees. However, the application allows for very large negative and positive degree values.

"rotate"
To default rotate an object:

```
rotate 20 90 -120;
```

Result: *The previously selected object(s) was rotated around the local X-axis 20 degrees, Y-axis 90 degrees, and Z-axis -120 degrees.*

Rotating objects is accomplished with three flags: *relative*, *absolute*, and *pivot*. By default, this method will rotate the currently selected object; if this previously-selected object is not to be rotated, a user can force the targeted object directly by calling for it. The "rotate" command can be paired with a select line or the name of the object can follow the orientation coordinates. Also, like the select command, this can operate on singular names, name lists and name arrays.

```
-r      or      -relative
-a      or      -absolute
-p      or      -pivot
```

Absolute Rotation
Absolute value flags are used when scripters rotate to a predetermined world space orientation.
To select an object and rotate it to an orientation in space…

```
select -r nurbsSphere1;
rotate -a 20 -40 120;
```

Result: *"nurbsSphere1" has been rotated to a new orientation around the local X-axis 20 degrees, local Y-axis -40 degrees and local Z-axis 120 degrees.*
To rotate an object to an orientation in space…

```
rotate -a 20 -40 120 nurbsSphere1;
```

Result: *"nurbsSphere1" has been rotated to a new orientation around the local X-axis 20 degrees, local Y-axis -40 degrees and local Z-axis 120 degrees. Note: "nurbsSphere1" did not need to be selected.*

Relative Rotation
Like translation, relative rotations are utilized when working more dynamically. The application will take the object and rotate it based on its current orientation.
To select an object and rotate relative to its current orientation…

```
select -r nurbsSphere1;
rotate -r 0 0 20;
```

Result: *"nurbsSphere1" has been rotated from its current orientation exactly 20 degrees more around the local Z axis.*

To rotate an object relative to its current orientation…

```
rotate -r 0 0 20 nurbsSphere1;
```

Result: *"nurbsSphere1" has been rotated from its current orientation exactly 20 degrees more around the local Z axis. Note: "nurbsSphere1" did not need to be selected.*

Pivot Position
For the previous cases, all examples are using the default pivot location. Without modification, typically this coincides with the centroid of the object. The default pivot is unique to each object, so when rotation occurs on two or more selected objects, each will rotate based on its respective axis system. This means each object is autonomous and unique, which is a great characteristic for dynamic aggregations.

However, the developers have provided a *pivot* flag to alter the rotation location. This has two benefits: the ability to rotate around an object, and the opportunity to pseudo-group collections of geometry to one centroid. These can be described best when referring to planetary orbits. The daily rotation of the earth illustrates a *default* rotation setting, and the orbiting motion of the moon around the earth showcases an example of rotation of an altered *pivot*.
To rotate an object *absolute* around a pivot axis…

```
rotate -p 3 -4 10 0 0 20 nurbsSphere1;
```

Result: *"nurbsSphere1" has been rotated to a new orientation exactly 20 degrees around the pivot Z axis located at the coordinate (3, -4, 10).*

To rotate two objects *absolute* around a pivot axis…

```
rotate -p 3 -4 10 0 0 20 nurbsSphere1 nurbsSphere2;
```

Result: *"nurbsSphere1" and "nurbsSphere2" have been rotated to a new orientation exactly 20 degrees around the pivot Z axis located at the coordinate (3, -4, 10).*

In the previous example with two (or more) objects, the use of pivot forces all participating objects to share the same axis coordinate. Pivot-less rotations will use the default, where each object has its own respective rotation.

To rotate an object *relative* around a pivot axis…

```
rotate -r -p 3 -4 10 0 0 20 nurbsSphere1;
```

Result: *"nurbsSphere1" has been rotated from its current orientation exactly 20 degrees more around the pivot Z axis located at the coordinate (3, -4, 10).*

To rotate two objects *relative* around a pivot axis...

```
rotate -r -p 3 -4 10 0 0 20 nurbsSphere1 nurbsSphere2;
```

Result: *"nurbsSphere1" and "nurbsSphere2" have been rotated from their current orientation exactly 20 degrees more around the pivot Z axis located at the coordinate (3, -4, 10).*

Scale
Scaling geometry is the process of resizing an object, based on three dimensions. Scalings require three float values in scalar units, corresponding to the local XYZ axis system. This states the object can be universally resized when the X, Y and Z are identical values, or the object can be squashed or extended in one direction with differing values. Just like the rotate command, the pivot location of the object is extremely important, because this establishes the anchor for size transformation. Unlike "rotate" and "move" where zero is the base number, scaling is contingent upon the value one. A scalar value of zero would flatten the object to an infinitesimally small thickness, prompting warning messages.

"scale"
To default scale an object:

```
scale 1.5 0.7 0.8;
```

Result: *The previously selected object(s) was scaled to a size of 1.5 in the X direction, 0.7 in the Y and 0.8 in the Z.*

Scaling objects is accomplished with three flags: *relative*, *absolute*, and *pivot*. By default, this method will resize the currently selected object, however a user can force the targeted object directly. The "scale" command can be paired with a select line or the name of the object can follow the scalar values. Also, like the select command, this can operate on singular names, name lists and name arrays.

```
-r      or      -relative
-a      or      -absolute
-p      or      -pivot
```

Absolute Scaling
Absolute value flags are used when scripters scale to a predetermined world space size.
To select an object and scale it to a size in space...

```
select -r nurbsSphere1;
scale -a 1.5 0.7 0.8;
```

Result: *"nurbsSphere1" has been scaled to a new size of 1.5 in the X direction, 0.7 in the Y and 0.8 in the Z.*

To scale an object to a size in space...

```
scale -a 1.5 0.7 0.8 nurbsSphere1;
```

Result: *"nurbsSphere1" has been scaled to a new size of 1.5 in the X direction, 0.7 in the Y and 0.8 in the Z. Note: "nurbsSphere1" did not need to be selected.*

Relative Scaling
Like translation and rotation, relative scalings are utilized when working more dynamically. The application will take the object and scale it based on its current size.
To select an object and scale relative to its current size...

```
select -r nurbsSphere1;
scale -r 1 1 12;
```

Result: *"nurbsSphere1" has been resized 12 times as large as its previous size in the Z direction. The X and Y directions were set to one, so no scaling occurred.*

To scale an object relative to its current size...

```
scale -r 1 1 12 nurbsSphere1;
```

Result: *"nurbsSphere1" has been resized 12 times as large as its previous size in the Z direction. The X and Y directions were set to one, so no scaling occurred. Note: "nurbsSphere1" did not need to be selected.*

Pivot Position
For the previous cases, all examples use the default pivot location. Without modification, typically this coincides with the centroid of the object. The default pivot is unique to each object, so when scaling occurs on two or more selected objects, each will resize based on its respective axis system. This means each object is autonomous and unique, which is a great characteristic for dynamic shaping.

Nearly identical to rotation positioning, the developers have provided a *pivot* flag to alter the scaling centroid location. The previous two benefits remain: the ability to resize an object from an outside coordinate, and the opportunity to pseudo-group collections of geometry to one centroid.
To scale an object *absolute* around a pivot axis...

```
scale -p 2 2 2 1 1 5.2 nurbsSphere1;
```

Result: *"nurbsSphere1" has been resized to 5.2 in the Z direction from the pivot coordinate (2, 2, 2). The X and Y directions were set to one, so no scaling occurred.*

To scale two objects *absolute* around a pivot axis...

```
scale -p 2 2 2 1 1 5.2 nurbsSphere1 nurbsSphere2;
```

Result: *"nurbsSphere1" and "nurbsSphere2" have been resized to 5.2 in the Z direction from the pivot coordinate (2, 2, 2). The X and Y directions were set to one, so no scaling occurred.*

To scale an object *relative* around a pivot axis...

```
scale -r -p -1.5 -1.5 -1.5 1 1 1.2 nurbsSphere1;
```

Result: *"nurbsSphere1" has been resized 1.2 times as large as its previous size in the Z direction from the pivot coordinate (-1.5, -1.5, -1.5). The X and Y directions were set to one, so no scaling occurred.*

To scale two objects *relative* around a pivot axis...

```
scale -r -p -1.5 -1.5 -1.5 1 1 1.2 nurbsSphere1 nurbsSphere2;
```

Result: *"nurbsSphere1" and "nurbsSphere2" have been resized 1.2 times as large as their previous size in the Z direction from the pivot coordinate (-1.5, -1.5, -1.5). The X and Y directions were set to one, so no scaling occurred.*

Xform Matrix

The *xform* command coalesces all of the translation, rotation, and scale methods into one. While "move," "rotate," and "scale" are perfectly viable means of modifying the transform information of an object, *xform* simplifies a coder's work. In one elegant statement, *xform* can replace the work of writing three separate lines of code for resizing, orienting, and translating an object in a sequence.

Each method has its own flag. "move" corresponds to −t, "rotate" relates to −ro and −s abbreviates "scale." As always, transform commands depend entirely on modification locations and current values. The flags for *relative, absolute, world space,* and *pivot* maintain their significance and must be combined to ensure proper dynamic behavior. The following examples pertain to a previously created object which is selected.

-t	or	-translate
-ro	or	-rotate
-s	or	-scale
-sh	or	-shear

```
-ws     or      -worldSpace
-r      or      -relative
-a      or      -absolute
-p      or      -pivot
```

```
xform -r -t 3 2 2;
xform -ws -t 0.9 2.2 8;
xform -r -ro 10 -10 10;
xform -ws -ro 70 20 110;
xform -r -s 1.4 0.6 0.8;
xform -ws -s 2.4 2.6 1.8;
```

In addition to the aforementioned methods, *xform* exposes the modification of objects by shearing. All objects have an invisible "bounding box" encapsulating the primitive. The *shear* attribute takes one side of the box and its respective opposite, and slides them from a rectangular solid into a parallelepiped. There is no singular command for shear; this can only be modified by *xform*.

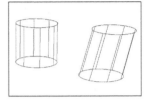

```
xform -r -sh 1.1 1.1 0.9;
xform -ws -sh 2 4 6;
```

Combining tasks can be accomplished two ways: by matrix or by adding flags. The matrix calculations are found in the command reference. Flag combination is far simpler for users just placing flags in succession. The only downside to task sequences is all operations must be either relative or world space, meaning a coder cannot rotate relative and scale absolutely.

```
xform -r -t 0.2 0.8 -0.1 -ro 10 10 10;
xform -ws -t 2 -10 -10 -ro 220 70 30;
xform -r -t 1 1 -1 -ro -10 15 8 -s 1.3 -0.8 -0.8;
```

Difference between Flag Position and Transform Position
For this and the previous chapter, this manual has presented two ways of creating geometry and placing it into a location. One technique is by using the primitive command and its pivot flag, while the other deals with creating a default object and using a transform command like move to place it in the desired location. On the surface, they appear to give identical, but misleading results. Take the example...

```
sphere -r 0.5 -p 10 10 10 -n "HH1";
```

or

```
sphere -r 0.5 "HH2";
move -ws 10 10 10 HH2;
```

Both HH1 and HH2 have a radius of 0.5 and reside at the coordinate (10, 10, 10). The difference is evident when you select the objects. HH1 will have a pivot not at the centroid of the sphere but rather at the origin, and HH2's pivot coincides with the centroid coordinate. Unless the coder is dealing with eccentric orientation and/or resizing, it is a best practice to always devote translation to the "move" command. This will be vital for proximity calculations in later chapters, because the pivot location often does not correspond to actual XYZ coordinate of the object.

Duplication

The last major command in the MEL library is the process of copying, called *duplicate*. In its default state, the duplication of an object may appear the same, but is not an identical reproduction. More flags can be found in the command reference, but this section will just explain the default and input connection attributes.

To make a default duplication of a sphere...

```
sphere -r 0.75 -n "SP1";
duplicate;
```

Result: *A sphere named "SP1" and a surface resembling a sphere named "SP2" was created.*

The previous example created a sphere and understanding all creation commands end with the last object selected, the duplication requires no input name string. If the object is not selected, the name of the duplicator must follow the *duplicate* command.

```
sphere -r 0.75 -n "SQ1";
select -cl;
duplicate SQ1;
```

Result: *A sphere named "SQ1" and a surface resembling a sphere named "SQ2" was created.*

As mentioned, there exist several flags for this command, however *name* and *input connection* are most pertinent at this level of expertise. The *name* deals with the output name of the duplication, and not the name of the input geometry to be duplicated. This is a common mistake. As usual, -n stands for the input string.

```
sphere -r 0.75 -n "SR1";
duplicate -n "KR1";
```

Result: *A sphere named "SR1" and a surface resembling a sphere named "KR1" was created.*

A pattern is emerging in the previous three result statements. "A surface resembling" takes the place of "sphere," even though in the viewport window, there appears two coincidental sphere shapes. This is an illusion. The duplicated object in default mode is not actually a sphere, but rather an imitation that copied the internal geometric NURBS information. Radius, end, and start sweep data (among other sphere-based values) are not exposed once a default duplication occurs.

If a coder wishes to restore and maintain the attributes of the object in a duplication, the inputConnections flag is a requirement. This connection, however, has limits, for it shares the link to the original sphere node.

```
sphere -r 0.75 -n "ST1";
duplicate -ic -n "KT1";
```

Result: *A sphere named "ST1" and a surface resembling a sphere named "KT1" was created.*

Chapter 8

Intelligent Repetition
Repetition versus Recursion
Manual Repetition
For and While Loops
>"for"
>**Repetitive "for" Loops**
>**Recursive "for" Loops**

"do...while"
>**Repetitive "do...while" Loops**
>**Recursive "do...while" Loops**
>**Ending "do...while" Conditionals Early**

Endless Loops
currentTime
Nesting Loops

Intelligent Repetition

Up until this page, all of the content in the previous chapters covered simple tasks or small sequences of commands. These procedures comprise the fundamentals of basic scripting and their syntax and format require mastering before undertaking more advanced techniques of automation. Once familiarity of these fundamentals is achieved, skeptics may inquire on the efficiency of computational design. To complete a simple sequence of tasks, almost a paragraph or page of text would need to be typed, executed, and maintained, when the use of the user-interface would simplify these procedures into a few clicks of a mouse.

Technically, coders could write out one line for each task. This would result in a direct relationship of the size of the code to the task count, and thusly be very inefficient. So if a user wanted to make one thousand spheres, the script would need to be one thousand lines long. In the field of three-dimensional modeling, more resolution triumphs; in computer programming, less is more.

The main goal in scripting, contrary to modeling, is to minimize the size of the script while still maintaining underlying intelligence. The primary mechanism for repetition and the most ubiquitous framework for all computer programming is the loop. Looping replays a desired sequence of code until an end condition is satisfied.

Repetition versus Recursion

Looping can be categorized as two types: repetitive and recursive. Repetitive scenarios simulate the process of mass production. Repetitive arrangements are instantiated from on an original master entity, like a variable, geometric construction, or other. One can look to the process of casting; there exists a master die which produces thousands of identical output objects. The results of the system are logical, identical and highly-predictable.

Recursive sequences build on the latest iteration of the loop. This structure appears similar to repetition, however the results of the system are less intuitive. There exist several ways to employ a recursive sequence, and this chapter will focus on geometric capabilities. Later chapters will discuss recursion in procedures and functions. Evolution exemplifies a recursive automation loop, because each agent in the loop passes down its generational traits to the newly created offspring.

Manual Repetition

Just for rhetorical purposes, consider the following. Without looping, scripting would be long and tedious. If a user wished to make ten NURBS toruses located in a line, the following lines would need to be authored:

```
torus -r 2 -hr 0.5 -s 8 -n "TTorus1";
move -r -10 0 0;
torus -r 2 -hr 0.5 -s 8 -n "TTorus2";
move -r -8 0 0;
torus -r 2 -hr 0.5 -s 8 -n "TTorus3";
move -r -6 0 0;
torus -r 2 -hr 0.5 -s 8 -n "TTorus4";
move -r -4 0 0;
torus -r 2 -hr 0.5 -s 8 -n "TTorus5";
move -r -2 0 0;
torus -r 2 -hr 0.5 -s 8 -n "TTorus6";
move -r 0 0 0;
torus -r 2 -hr 0.5 -s 8 -n "TTorus7";
move -r 2 0 0;
torus -r 2 -hr 0.5 -s 8 -n "TTorus8";
move -r 4 0 0;
torus -r 2 -hr 0.5 -s 8 -n "TTorus9";
move -r 6 0 0;
torus -r 2 -hr 0.5 -s 8 -n "TTorus10";
move -r 8 0 0;
```

This example displays poor scripting practice, for there should be little or no text repetition in a script. Loops should be utilized to minimize the length of the code whenever possible.

Looping allows a coder to establish a start assignment, end condition and interval for sequenced commands. To replicate the aforementioned example with loops, the infrastructure should follow this framework:

Beginning Value
    {   Repeated Code Sequence }
End Value

The initial condition establishes a start number and the end sets up the last number in the sequence. These could be any float which determines the count. As the loop increases or decreases the "counter," the end condition is satisfied. In the rhetorical example above, the beginning and end values would be 1 and 10 respectively.

The block of repeated code would be the following. Note: the character "X" denotes a place where the values must change in accordance to the counter.

```
torus -r 2 -hr 0.5 -s 8 -n "TTorusX";
move -r X 0 0;
```

If these two lines where placed in a loop, the previous twenty lines in the rhetorical example could be replaced with a concise four line loop. The next sections in this chapter explain the syntax and potential of repetition in scripting.

For and While Loops
Loops can be constructed in two ways. One method is called the "for" loop and deals with equal incremental changes with an explicit beginning and end condition. The other looping method stops at a desired conditional test and is called a "while" loop. All loops encapsulate the repeated code in braces   { } and logic tests precede or follow.

"For" loops are small but esoteric, and "while" loops are long but didactic. Both can be employed for the same task repetition, but the coder should determine which method suits him or her best. "While" loops exhibit more functionality than "for" statements for advanced topics, which will be covered later in this chapter.

To explain this more clearly, think of a loop as a Ferris Wheel. As riders fill the baskets, an operator pulls a lever to begin the rotation of the wheel (*Start Condition*). Riders may circle the several times (*Interval*) until the operator begins the process of unloading (*End Condition*). Since the supervisor operates outside of the system, he/she dictates the End Condition, and the agents riding the wheel play no role in the stopping of the machine. This is the logic of the "for" loop.

"While" loops are like a Ferris Wheel, but slightly different. Imagine the supervisor of the wheel decided to invent a remote control to drive the Ferris Wheel. He/she could ride with the occupants of the wheel and start and end the machine based upon face-to-face reactions of the riders. If the occupants are excited and positive, the operator could decide to let the ride last longer. If some occupants are upset or scared, the supervisor could decrease the number of revolutions. This defines the "while" statement; the loop can be shut down inside of the process.

Regardless of "for" or "while," the Ferris Wheel analogy describes the process of repeating internal commands. Consider the events affecting an occupant of the ride and equate them to commands in a script. For the sake of argument, we will invent three new commands: "wave," "sightsee," and "vocalize." With each cycle of the wheel, the occupants begin near the bottom and elevate. They wave three times as they ascend and stop at the top to sightsee to the left side of the carnival for ten seconds. Lastly, their descent is punctuated with a loud vocalization to their friends with the statement "Hey!" The cycle repeats itself with each complete rotation until ten passes have been made. In concept, we can construct a pseudo-loop with these fictitious methods...

```
Beginning Value = 0
(
    wave -count 3;
    sightsee -left 10sec;
    vocalize -volume "loud" -target $FriendsList[2:8] -string "Hey!";
{
End Value = 10
```

This is a conceptual example where the commands are fictitious but the syntax and command order are essentially correct. This loop is false (pseudo-code), but shows how a scripter can encapsulate the repetitive tasks of enjoying a carnival ride into five simple lines of code.

for
The "for" loop syntax...

```
for ( Beginning Value ; End Value ; Interval ) {
        // Place Code Here...
}
```

An example of a "for" loop...

```
for ($i=1;$i<10;$i++) {
        print ("Current Loop Number:  " + $i + ".  ");
}
```

Result: *The History Window prints: "Current Loop Number: 1. Current Loop Number: 2. Current Loop Number: 3. Current Loop Number: 4. Current Loop Number: 5. Current Loop Number: 6. Current Loop Number: 7. Current Loop Number: 8. Current Loop Number: 9."*

- `$i`   All loops require a "counter" as a variable. This variable, either a float or integer, keeps track of the changing count.
- `$i=1;`   In the example, $i=1 determines the beginning. Variable $i could begin with any positive or negative integer or float. i.e. `$i=-120;` `$i=3240;` etc.

- $i<10;   Also, $i<10 sets a final conditional.   When programmers write these statements, they state to themselves, "If the current variable is less than X, continue. If not, stop." If the user wishes to stop exactly on 10, use $i<=10;

- $i++;   Using an additive operator, ++ will add one for each instance of the loop. The use of -- will subtract one from the current value counter.

Loops can begin with values other than zero or one. Also, these can end with the exact value of the final condition with the use of the less-than-and-equal-to operator.

Another example of a "for" loop...

```
for ($j=50;$j<=58;$j++) {
        print ("Current Loop Number:   " + $j + ".   ");
}
```

Result: *The History Window prints: "Current Loop Number: 50. Current Loop Number: 51. Current Loop Number: 52. Current Loop Number: 53. Current Loop Number: 54. Current Loop Number: 55. Current Loop Number: 56. Current Loop Number: 57. Current Loop Number: 58."*

Loops can also repeat geometric methods and change variables. In the example below, the counter ($k) starts at 1 and ends before 301, updates a variable ($DistX) with multiplication, and generates a sphere in space.

```
for ($k=1;$k<301;$k++) {
        float $DistX = 30*$k;
        sphere -r 2.25 -n ("SPHR" + $k);
        move -ws $DistX 0 0;
}
```

Result: *300 NURBS spheres are created in a row 30 units apart, with names beginning with "SPHR1," "SPHR2," "SPHR3," ... "SPHR300."*

Another geometry loop example with *move*, *rotate*, and *scale*...

```
for ($HHCounter=0;$HHCounter<155;$HHCounter++) {
   float $DX = 3 * $HHCounter;
   polyCube -w 4 -h 3 -d 2 -sx 3 -sy 4 -sz 5 -n ("PC" + $HHCounter);
   move -ws ($DX-77) 0 5;
   rotate -a $DX $DX 0;
   scale -a 1 1 0.88;
}
```

Result: *155 polygonalized cubes are created in a row 3 units apart, 3-degree interval rotation, and 0.88 z-scale, with names beginning with "PC0," "PC1," "PC2," ... "PC154."*

Repetitive "for" Loops

The previous "for" loops dealt with the creation of a series of objects and altering their transformation attributes. This technique is useful for setting up the file with construction geometry. Often times, however, scripters want to set up a generative process from a starter object (or collection/group of objects). This construction, called a repetitive loop, appears slightly different than the aforementioned examples, even though they seem nearly identical. The main difference between creation and repetitive loops is the addition of the "duplicate" command and the placement of the creation operation.

Repetitive loops usually begin with of the creation of a object or an start with an existing geometric object. Naming is crucial, because all duplication inside the loop will reference the starter object. This code will duplicate the position and orientation of the starter object, and the loop counter must modify the location, rotation and scale accordingly. Then the duplication records this modified location. The following example moves the starter object "NObj1" incrementally in the X direction, and with each revolution of the loop, a copy is made.

A geometry loop example duplicating the starter object "NObj1"…

```
sphere -r 2.25 -n "NObj1";
for ($V3=0;$V3<75;$V3++) {
        float $DX = 0.6 * $V3;
        duplicate "NObj1";
        move -ws ($DX-5) 0 7 "NObj1";
}
```

Result: *75 NURBS spheres are created in a row 0.6 units apart with names beginning with "NObj2," "NObj3," "NObj4," … "NObj75."*

Recursive "for" Loops

There exists another method of automated duplication, called recursive looping. Whereas repetitive loops copy the characteristics of a starter object, recursive loops use the previously created object as the lead duplicator. Repetition requires precise naming, but recursion requires precise sequencing. Understanding the application always selects the newly-created geometry after a duplication, the shape is primed for this type of copying.

A recursive geometry loop example…

```
sphere -r 2.25 -n "NH1";
for ($U_8=0;$U_8<59;$U_8++) {
        duplicate;
        move -ws ($U_8*2) 0 0;
}
```

Result: *59 NURBS spheres are created in a row 2 units apart with names beginning with "NH2," "NH3," "NH4," … "NH60."*

The previous example's result may appear to be very similar to the repetitive example. The identical linear outcome stems from the use of the world space flags for modification. All previous examples in this chapter utilized either world space or absolute flags, which require dynamic variables to generate variation. To work in a recursive mode, the use of relative flags yields more complex patterning.

A relative recursive geometry loop example…

```
sphere -r 2.25 -n "NH1";
for ($U_8=0;$U_8<59;$U_8++) {
      duplicate;
      move -r 3 0 0;
}
```

Result: *59 NURBS spheres are created in a row 3 units apart with names beginning with "NH2," "NH3," "NH4," … "NH60."*

A relative recursive geometry loop example with an increasing interstitial distance…

```
sphere -r 2.25 -n "NH1";
for ($U_8=0;$U_8<59;$U_8++) {
      duplicate;
      move -r $U_8 0 0;
}
```

Result: *59 NURBS spheres are created in a row with an ever-increasing distance between objects with names beginning with "NH2," "NH3," "NH4," … "NH60."*

When combining all of the transformation commands (*move, rotate* and *scale*) with relative configurations, extraordinary effects result. Relative rotations force the lead object into arching and sinuous paths. While *rotate* and *move* provide exciting and dynamic linear forms, *scale* operations must be handled in a delicate manner. It is recommended, but not a restriction, that recursive scalings should hover between values of 0.95 and 1.05. Understanding recursion builds on previous objects, it only takes a small sequence of duplications before the exponentially increasing or decreasing scale attribute value approximates zero or infinity. A zero thickness is technically possible with NURBS modeling, but this geometry is difficult to render, export or modify. An infinite, or extremely large, scaling forces the object to the extents of the model space, which may prove undesirable.

A relative recursive geometry loop example with more transformation commands…

```
sphere -r 2.25 -n "NH1";
for ($U_8=0;$U_8<59;$U_8++) {
      duplicate;
      move -r $U_8 2 0.7;
      rotate -r -os 10 10 121;
```

```
    scale -r 0.98 0.95 1.02;
}
```

Result: *59 NURBS spheres are created in an arched row with an ever-increasing distance between objects with names beginning with "NH2," "NH3," "NH4," ... "NH60."*

"do...while"

Looping with the "do...while" statement is clearer than "for." Instead of abbreviating the beginning, end, and interval values into one line, "do...while" syntax breaks apart each element into a linear sequence. One line is devoted to the beginning assignment, one line controls the end conditional, and one line increases the interval. This format tends to lend itself better for beginner coders, while expert programmers seem to implement "for" loops for most scenarios. The "while" loop syntax...

```
int Beginning Value
do {
        // Place Code Here...
        Interval
} while (End Value Condition)
```

An example of a "while" loop...

```
int $i=1;
do {
        print ("Current Loop Number:   " + $i + ".   ");
        $i++;
} while ($i < 10);
```

Result: *The History Window prints: "Current Loop Number: 1. Current Loop Number: 2. Current Loop Number: 3. Current Loop Number: 4. Current Loop Number: 5. Current Loop Number: 6. Current Loop Number: 7. Current Loop Number: 8. Current Loop Number: 9."*

- `$i`   All loops require a "counter" as a variable. This variable, either a float or integer, keeps track of the changing count. In "while" loops, this is an explicitly declared variable assigned prior outside the braces.
- `int $i=1;`   In the example, $i=1 determines the beginning. Variable $i could begin with any positive or negative value. i.e. $i=-120; $i=3240; etc. The example declares an integer, but floats can be employed as well.
- `$i++;`   Using an additive operator, ++ will add one for each instance of the loop. The use of -- will subtract one from the current value counter. For "while" loops, this operation must occur inside the braces.
- `while ($i<10);` Also, $i<10 sets a final conditional.   When programmers write these statements, they state to themselves, "If the current

variable is less than X, continue. If not, stop." If the user wishes to stop exactly on 10, use $i<=10;

"While" loops can begin with values other than zero or one. Also, these can end with the exact value of the final condition with the use of the less-than-and-equal-to operator.

Another example of a "while" loop...

```
int $j = 50;
do {
        print ("Current Loop Number:   " + $j + ".   ");
        $j++;
} while ($j<=58);
```

Result: *The History Window prints: "Current Loop Number: 50. Current Loop Number: 51. Current Loop Number: 52. Current Loop Number: 53. Current Loop Number: 54. Current Loop Number: 55. Current Loop Number: 56. Current Loop Number: 57. Current Loop Number: 58."*

Like "for" loops, "while" statements can also repeat geometric methods and change variables. In the example below, the counter ($k) starts at 1 and ends before 301, updates a variable ($DistX) with multiplication, and generates a sphere in space.

```
int $k = 1;
do {
        float $DistX = 30*$k;
        sphere -r 2.25 -n ("SPHR" + $k);
        move -ws $DistX 0 0;
        $k++;
} while ($k < 301);
```

Result: *300 NURBS spheres are created in a row 30 units apart, with names beginning with "SPHR1," "SPHR2," "SPHR3," ... "SPHR300."*

Another geometry loop example with *move*, *rotate*, and *scale*...

```
int $HHCounter = 0;
do {
   float $DX = 3 * $HHCounter;
   polyCube -w 4 -h 3 -d 2 -sx 3 -sy 4 -sz 5 -n ("PC" + $HHCounter);
   move -ws ($DX-77) 0 5;
   rotate -a $DX $DX 0;
   scale -a 1 1 0.88;
   $HHCounter++;
} while ($HHCounter < 155);
```

Result: *155 polygonalized cubes are created in a row 3 units apart, 3-degree interval rotation, and 0.88 z-scale, with names beginning with "PC0," "PC1," "PC2," ... "PC154."*

Repetitive "do...while" Loops
This section is a variation on the topic of *"Repetitive 'for' Loops."* The following example moves the starter object "NObj1" incrementally in the X direction, and with each revolution of the loop, a copy is made.
A geometry loop example duplicating the starter object "NObj1"...

```
sphere -r 2.25 -n "NObj1";
int $V3 = 0;
do {
      float $DX = 0.6 * $V3;
      duplicate "NObj1";
      move -ws ($DX-5) 0 7 "NObj1";
      $V3++;
) while ($V3 < 75);
```

Result: *75 NURBS spheres are created in a row 0.6 units apart with names beginning with "NObj2," "NObj3," "NObj4," ... "NObj75."*

Recursive "do...while" Loops
This section is a variation on the topic of *"Recursive 'for' Loops."*
A recursive geometry loop example...

```
sphere -r 2.25 -n "NH1";
int $U_8 = 0;
do {
      duplicate;
      move -ws ($U_8*2) 0 0;
      $U_8++;
} while ($U_8 < 59);
```

Result: *59 NURBS spheres are created in a row 2 units apart with names beginning with "NH2," "NH3," "NH4," ... "NH60."*

To work in a recursive mode, the use of relative flags yields more complex patterning.
A relative recursive geometry loop example...

```
sphere -r 2.25 -n "NH1";
int $U_8 = 0;
do {
      duplicate;
      move -r 3 0 0;
      $U_8++;
} while ($U_8 < 59);
```

Result: *59 NURBS spheres are created in a row 3 units apart with names beginning with "NH2," "NH3," "NH4," ... "NH60."*

A relative recursive geometry loop example with an increasing interstitial distance...

```
sphere -r 2.25 -n "NH1";
int $U_8 = 0;
do {
        duplicate;
        move -r $U_8 0 0;
        $U_8++;
} while ($U_8 < 59);
```

Result: *59 NURBS spheres are created in a row with an ever-increasing distance between objects with names beginning with "NH2," "NH3," "NH4," ... "NH60."*

A relative recursive geometry loop example with more transformation commands...

```
sphere -r 2.25 -n "NH1";
int $U_8 = 0;
do {
        duplicate;
        move -r $U_8 2 0.7;
        rotate -r -os 10 10 121;
        scale -r 0.98 0.95 1.02;
        $U_8++;
} while ($U_8 < 59);
```

Result: *59 NURBS spheres are created in an arched row with an ever-increasing distance between objects with names beginning with "NH2," "NH3," "NH4," ... "NH60."*

Ending "do...while" Conditionals Early
Early this chapter, a metaphor was constructed to distinguish "for" from "while" loops. In the case of the "while" statement, a Ferris wheel had an operator with a remote control. This enabled the driver to ride with the occupants and determine the end of the loop internally.

The previous "do...while" examples all simulated the original "for" loops exactly to display that both methodologies can produce identical results. However, "while" loops have an added benefit. Knowing they are controlled by a conditional, any manner of logical fitness will discontinue the automation process. A counter may or may not occupy the "while" loop syntax.

An example of a loop which stops randomly...

```
sphere -r 2.25 -n "NH1";
float $URand;
int $U_8 = 0;
do {
        duplicate;
        move -r $U_8 2 0.7;
        rotate -r -os 10 10 121;
```

```
        scale -r 0.98 0.95 1.02;
        $URand = rand(0,40);
} while ($URand > 2);
```

Result: *An unpredictable quantity of duplicated spheres are created in an arc.*
The probability of ending the loop is 1 in 40.

In most cases, and as a best practice, any non-counter "do…while" loop should
use gates to ensure a controlled end condition. As a typical way of maintaining
a check on possible rogue endless loops, coders often employ a secondary end
condition using a basic max counter. Without combining a non-counter end
condition with a basic maximum count, scripts can theoretically run forever.
An example of a loop which stops randomly and has a max count…

```
sphere -r 2.25 -n "NH1";
float $URand;
int $U_8 = 0;
int $Ucount = 0
do {
        duplicate;
        move -r $U_8 2 0.7;
        rotate -r -os 10 10 121;
        scale -r 0.98 0.95 1.02;
        $URand = rand(0,40);
        $Ucount++;
} while ($URand > 2 && $Ucount < 100);
```

Result: *An unpredictable quantity of duplicated spheres are created in an arc.*
The probability of ending the loop is 1 in 40 as long as no more than 99 spheres
were created..

Endless Loops
All loops have a beginning, end, and interval value. However, in the process of
scripting, it is common to make a typo or forget important characters or words.
With all computer programming, correct syntax is paramount, but loops require
extra attention. Maya has an unfortunate dysfunctionality where running MEL
scripts cannot be stopped. If a coder has forgotten to add the interval or made an
impossible end condition, the script will run endlessly until the application
crashes or is manually shut down.

If a scripter has forgotten to place the ++ operator, the code always stays at the
initial counter value. It never reaches the end condition, resulting in an endless
loop.
An example of a common endless loop mistake (forgotten interval operation)…

Incorrect:
```
// WARNING: Endless loop example.  Do not run. //
int $U_8 = 0;
do {
        print ("Value:  " + $U_8);
```

```
} while ($U_8 < 59);
// WARNING: Endless loop example.  Do not run. //
```

Result: *The application stalls and must be forced close.*

Correct:
```
int $U_8 = 0;
do {
      print ("Value:   " + $U_8);
      $U_8++;
} while ($U_8 < 59);
```

Coders sometimes wish to have an increment interval of less than one. This means the counter declaration must be a float, otherwise the increment will always truncate to the initial counter value.
Another example of a common endless loop mistake (wrong counter data-type)…

Incorrect:
```
// WARNING: Endless loop example.  Do not run. //
int $HCounter = 0;
do {
      print ("Value:   " + $HCounter);
      $HCounter=$HCounter + 0.1;
} while ($HCounter < 10);
// WARNING: Endless loop example.  Do not run. //
```

Result: *The application stalls and must be forced close.*

Correct:
```
float $HCounter = 0;
do {
      print ("Value:   " + $HCounter);
      $HCounter=$HCounter + 0.1;
} while ($HCounter < 10);
```

"currentTime"
For all previous loops, there was no means of refreshing the display and visualizing until the final output of the script. For a standard loop, once the code was executed, moments and sometimes minutes would pass until its completion. Then magically, the geometry appears as a completed assembly of objects. This is the preferred means of automation, because it requires the least amount of memory and it allocates the entire computing capacity to just calculating the code.

It is often important for learning purposes and specialized cases to see the model refresh at a moment in time for debugging or presentation visualization. To accomplish this, the use of the command "currentTime" is best. This command is best known for moving the timeslider to a frame (see the next chapter for more information), but it also refreshes the display. When a scripter makes a loop with this command, for each cycle of automation, the screen updates to display the newly modified or created geometry.

A relative recursive geometry loop example with transformation commands and display refreshing…

```
sphere -r 2.25 -n "NH1";
int $U_8 = 0;
do {
        duplicate;
        move -r $U_8 2 0.7;
        rotate -r -os 10 10 121;
        scale -r 0.98 0.95 1.02;
        currentTime $U_8;
        $U_8++;
} while ($U_8 < 59);
```

Result: *Visualized over a few seconds, 59 NURBS spheres are created individually in an arched row with an ever-increasing distance between objects with names beginning with "NH2," "NH3," "NH4," ... "NH60."*

A relative recursive geometry loop example with transformation commands and display refreshing…

```
sphere -r 2.25 -n "NH1";
for ($U_8=0;$U_8<59;$U_8++) {
        duplicate;
        move -r $U_8 2 0.7;
        rotate -r -os 10 10 121;
        scale -r 0.98 0.95 1.02;
        currentTime $U_8;
}
```

Result: *Visualized over a few seconds, 59 NURBS spheres are created individually in an arched row with an ever-increasing distance between objects with names beginning with "NH2," "NH3," "NH4," ... "NH60."*

Nesting Loops
There exist two ways of combining loops to produce optimal effects: sequential and nested. When combining loops in sequence, this can be explained as an additive way of automating. Once Loop 1 has completed, then Loop 2 begins, then Loop 3 and so on. Nesting loops is a multiplicative means of automation. When Loops 1 begins, it runs the entirety of Loop2 before moving onto the next instance of Loop 1. This process is repeated until Loop 1 has been exhausted.

The process of nesting loops allows scripters to make multiple degrees of complexity. For example, if the desired outcome is to make a 10x10 square grid of spheres, one loop would not suffice. One inefficient solution is to make ten sequential loops.

```
// Sequential loop example.  Very inefficient & not to be used.
for ($i=0;$i<10;$i++) {
        sphere -r 1.25 -n "NH1";
        move -ws ($i*2) 0 0;
        currentTime $i;
}
for ($i=0;$i<10;$i++) {
        sphere -r 1.25 -n "NH1";
        move -ws ($i*2) 2 0;
        currentTime $i;
}
for ($i=0;$i<10;$i++) {
        sphere -r 1.25 -n "NH1";
        move -ws ($i*2) 4 0;
        currentTime $i;
}
for ($i=0;$i<10;$i++) {
        sphere -r 1.25 -n "NH1";
        move -ws ($i*2) 6 0;
        currentTime $i;
}
for ($i=0;$i<10;$i++) {
        sphere -r 1.25 -n "NH1";
        move -ws ($i*2) 8 0;
        currentTime $i;
}
for ($i=0;$i<10;$i++) {
        sphere -r 1.25 -n "NH1";
        move -ws ($i*2) 10 0;
        currentTime $i;
}
for ($i=0;$i<10;$i++) {
        sphere -r 1.25 -n "NH1";
        move -ws ($i*2) 12 0;
        currentTime $i;
}
for ($i=0;$i<10;$i++) {
        sphere -r 1.25 -n "NH1";
        move -ws ($i*2) 14 0;
        currentTime $i;
}
for ($i=0;$i<10;$i++) {
        sphere -r 1.25 -n "NH1";
        move -ws ($i*2) 16 0;
        currentTime $i;
}
for ($i=0;$i<10;$i++) {
        sphere -r 1.25 -n "NH1";
        move -ws ($i*2) 18 0;
        currentTime $i;
}
//Not to be used.
```

Result: *Visualized over a few seconds, a grid of spheres in the X and Y directions is created.*

A more appropriate use of code is to make one loop for the Y direction of spheres nested inside another loop for the X direction.
To make a 10x10 grid of spheres...

```
for ($i=0;$i<10;$i++) {
        for ($j=0;$j<10;$j++) {
                sphere -r 1.25 -n "NH1";
                move -ws ($i*2) ($j*2) 0;
        currentTime $j;
        }
}
```

Result: *Visualized over a few seconds, a grid of spheres in the X and Y directions is created.*

As you can see, both codes produce the same results. One is fifty-two lines long (sequential) and the other is seven (nested). As with all computer programming, the size of a script is inversely indicative of its intelligence. In this case, the nested loop is more appropriate.

Another loop can be nested inside the previous nested loop, generating a cube of spheres. The innermost loop controls the translate value for the Z direction, while X and Y are manipulated by the first and middle loops.
To make a 10x10x10 cubic volume of spheres...

```
for ($i=0;$i<10;$i++) {
        for ($j=0;$j<10;$j++) {
                for ($k=0;$k<10;$k++) {
                        sphere -r 1.25 -n "NH1";
                        move -ws ($i*2) ($j*2) ($k*2);
                        currentTime $k;
                }
        }
}
```

Result: *Visualized over a few seconds, a cube of spheres in the X, Y, and Z directions is created.*

The number of nested loops can be nearly infinite. If working geometrically, nesting is usually limited to three dimensions, but other bits of data can be applied to each object. Building Information Modeling is a term used in the architecture and engineering industries when applying data for construction quantities and scheduling. In the field of visual effects, adding data for visualization, keyframing, rendering or sequencing is referred to as Animation Setup.

The next chapters will explore these "extra dimensions" which either break down or are characteristics of objects. Chapter 9 will show every object retains global and unique traits called attributes. Each object can be disassembled into several modifiable and readable control manipulators, as will be revealed in Chapter 10.   Chapter 11 will discuss the ability to link these attributes and manipulators to the timeline, which is called keyframing.   Lastly, the final characteristic of all virtual objects is the materiality and visualization values. This culminates with process of rendering, which will be uncovered in Chapter 12.

Chapter 9

Querying and Setting Information

All primitives hold embedded information that can be unlocked or retrieved at any time. This data is managed in a system called nodes and accessed through attributes. Every object has between two and five initial nodes, and each node can house zero to hundreds of attributes.

Nodes and attributes can be likened to the dashboard of an automobile. Each dashboard is different for each vehicle make and model, much like each primitive's node composition is unique. Also, each car dashboard is divided into categories for the radio, gauges, and climate consoles, which are comparable to nodes of a primitive. Lastly and analogous to attributes, each console is broken down into specific gauges and buttons. Some gauges are "read-only," like the temperature or oil pressure indicators, and some buttons are interactive, or "writable," like the radio volume and heater fan speed. Navigating attributes requires a solid understanding of which characteristics are "read-only" or "writable and readable."

Sample Starter Code

When learning about setting and getting attributes, we require a scene populated with objects. It is not possible to read attributes on objects that do not exist. All of the examples for the remainder of this chapter will require the execution of this script ("CODE 9A") first:

```
// CODE 9A //
int $SCounter = 0;
sphere -r 1.25 -n "NS1";
do {
        //Recursive Loop
        duplicate;
        move -r $SCounter 2 0.7;
        rotate -r -os 10 10 121;
        $SCounter++;
} while ($SCounter < 59);
int $PCounter = 0;
do {
        //Pivot Loop
        float $eswV = (90+16*$PCounter);
        float $pY = (2*sin($PCounter));
        torus -p $PCounter $pY 5 -d 3 -esw $eswV -r 1 -hr 0.5;
        $PCounter++;
} while ($PCounter < 52);
```

Backticks

In Chapter 5, backticks were used to return queried geometry by immediately evaluating the edit command. This same character will be utilized to return attribute data. As a reminder, the backtick is the character below the "Esc" key and looks like this: `

A common mistake is use the apostrophe key (" ' "); errors will result if backticks are missing or misused. Review Chapter 5 for more information on backticks.

Lists (ls)

Before diving into attributes and nodes, coders need to know how to manage large lists of objects or characteristics. The best way to accomplish this is to store collections of names in string arrays, called *lists*. The universal command "ls" can produce several filtered lists based on string and flag configurations. By combining flags with wildcards, users can retrieve the diverse populations of primitives in an existing scene.

The list of flags is rather extensive, but to simplify instruction, this manual will cover only five configurations. Listed below, these will search for selected objects (-sl), cameras (-ca), visible objects (-v), transform node names (-tr) and all objects (no flag). More flags can be found in the command reference and later chapters will supplement this list.

```
ls;
ls -sl;
```

```
ls -ca;
ls -v;
ls -tr;
```

A flag-less "ls" command is completely unfiltered. Even with an empty or new file, there are several "objects" residing in the scene. To generate a complete list of objects and save those names into a string array…

```
string $AllArr[] = `ls`;
```

```
// Result: time1 renderPartition renderGlobalsList1 defaultLightList1 defaultShaderList1
postProcessList1 defaultRenderUtilityList1 lightList1 defaultTextureList1 lambert1
particleCloud1 initialShadingGroup initialParticleSE initialMaterialInfo shaderGlow1 dof1
defaultRenderGlobals defaultRenderQuality defaultResolution defaultLightSet
defaultObjectSet hardwareRenderGlobals characterPartition defaultHardwareRenderGlobals
ikSystem hyperGraphInfo hyperGraphLayout globalCacheControl dynController1 persp
perspShape top topShape front frontShape side sideShape lightLinker1 brush1 strokeGlobals
layersFilter objectTypeFilter52 renderLayersFilter objectTypeFilter53 renderingSetsFilter
objectTypeFilter54 relationshipPanel1LeftAttrFilter relationshipPanel1RightAttrFilter
layerManager defaultLayer renderLayerManager defaultRenderLayer globalRender NS1 NS1Shape
makeNurbSphere1 NS2 NS2Shape NS3 NS3Shape NS4 NS4Shape NS5 NS5Shape NS6 NS6Shape NS7
NS7Shape NS8 NS8Shape NS9 NS9Shape NS10 NS10Shape NS11 NS11Shape NS12 NS12Shape NS13
NS13Shape NS14 NS14Shape NS15 NS15Shape NS16 NS16Shape NS17 NS17Shape NS18 NS18Shape NS19
NS19Shape NS20 NS20Shape NS21 NS21Shape NS22 NS22Shape NS23 NS23Shape NS24 NS24Shape NS25
NS25Shape NS26 NS26Shape NS27 NS27Shape NS28 NS28Shape NS29 NS29Shape NS30 NS30Shape NS31
NS31Shape NS32 NS32Shape NS33 NS33Shape NS34 NS34Shape NS35 NS35Shape NS36 NS36Shape NS37
NS37Shape NS38 NS38Shape NS39 NS39Shape NS40 NS40Shape NS41 NS41Shape NS42 NS42Shape NS43
NS43Shape NS44 NS44Shape NS45 NS45Shape NS46 NS46Shape NS47 NS47Shape NS48 NS48Shape NS49
NS49Shape NS50 NS50Shape NS51 NS51Shape NS52 NS52Shape NS53 NS53Shape NS54 NS54Shape NS55
NS55Shape NS56 NS56Shape NS57 NS57Shape NS58 NS58Shape NS59 NS59Shape NS60 NS60Shape
nurbsTorus1 nurbsTorusShape1 makeNurbTorus1 nurbsTorus2 nurbsTorusShape2 makeNurbTorus2
nurbsTorus3 nurbsTorusShape3 makeNurbTorus3 nurbsTorus4 nurbsTorusShape4 makeNurbTorus4
nurbsTorus5 nurbsTorusShape5 makeNurbTorus5 nurbsTorus6 nurbsTorusShape6 makeNurbTorus6
nurbsTorus7 nurbsTorusShape7 makeNurbTorus7 nurbsTorus8 nurbsTorusShape8 makeNurbTorus8
nurbsTorus9 nurbsTorusShape9 makeNurbTorus9 nurbsTorus10 nurbsTorusShape10
makeNurbTorus10 nurbsTorus11 nurbsTorusShape11 makeNurbTorus11 nurbsTorus12
nurbsTorusShape12 makeNurbTorus12 nurbsTorus13 nurbsTorusShape13 makeNurbTorus13
nurbsTorus14 nurbsTorusShape14 makeNurbTorus14 nurbsTorus15 nurbsTorusShape15
makeNurbTorus15 nurbsTorus16 nurbsTorusShape16 makeNurbTorus16 nurbsTorus17
nurbsTorusShape17 makeNurbTorus17 nurbsTorus18 nurbsTorusShape18 makeNurbTorus18
nurbsTorus19 nurbsTorusShape19 makeNurbTorus19 nurbsTorus20 nurbsTorusShape20
makeNurbTorus20 nurbsTorus21 nurbsTorusShape21 makeNurbTorus21 nurbsTorus22
nurbsTorusShape22 makeNurbTorus22 nurbsTorus23 nurbsTorusShape23 makeNurbTorus23
nurbsTorus24 nurbsTorusShape24 makeNurbTorus24 nurbsTorus25 nurbsTorusShape25
makeNurbTorus25 nurbsTorus26 nurbsTorusShape26 makeNurbTorus26 nurbsTorus27
nurbsTorusShape27 makeNurbTorus27 nurbsTorus28 nurbsTorusShape28 makeNurbTorus28
nurbsTorus29 nurbsTorusShape29 makeNurbTorus29 nurbsTorus30 nurbsTorusShape30
makeNurbTorus30 nurbsTorus31 nurbsTorusShape31 makeNurbTorus31 nurbsTorus32
nurbsTorusShape32 makeNurbTorus32 nurbsTorus33 nurbsTorusShape33 makeNurbTorus33
nurbsTorus34 nurbsTorusShape34 makeNurbTorus34 nurbsTorus35 nurbsTorusShape35
makeNurbTorus35 nurbsTorus36 nurbsTorusShape36 makeNurbTorus36 nurbsTorus37
nurbsTorusShape37 makeNurbTorus37 nurbsTorus38 nurbsTorusShape38 makeNurbTorus38
nurbsTorus39 nurbsTorusShape39 makeNurbTorus39 nurbsTorus40 nurbsTorusShape40
makeNurbTorus40 nurbsTorus41 nurbsTorusShape41 makeNurbTorus41 nurbsTorus42
nurbsTorusShape42 makeNurbTorus42 nurbsTorus43 nurbsTorusShape43 makeNurbTorus43
nurbsTorus44 nurbsTorusShape44 makeNurbTorus44 nurbsTorus45 nurbsTorusShape45
makeNurbTorus45 nurbsTorus46 nurbsTorusShape46 makeNurbTorus46 nurbsTorus47
nurbsTorusShape47 makeNurbTorus47 nurbsTorus48 nurbsTorusShape48 makeNurbTorus48
nurbsTorus49 nurbsTorusShape49 makeNurbTorus49 nurbsTorus50 nurbsTorusShape50
makeNurbTorus50 nurbsTorus51 nurbsTorusShape51 makeNurbTorus51 nurbsTorus52
nurbsTorusShape52 makeNurbTorus52 //
```

An unfiltered list is quite large, even for this relatively small scene. The command always structures the list in order of creation. The first fifty-two names pertain to file specific objects like rendering settings, default materials, camera names, and other required items. All latter objects were generated by the code.

The next lines can be used to make string arrays of important subsets of the scene...

```
string $SelArr[] = `ls -sl`;
string $CamArr[] = `ls -ca`;
string $VizArr[] = `ls -v`;
string $TrArr[] = `ls -tr`;
```

The selection flag is undoubtedly the most used and important filter for the list command. This will return any current selected object name or list of names. A cleared selection will return an empty array. Several commands generally leave the newly created primitive or operation highlighted, therefore using the selection filter can return names for future opportunities.

```
string $SelArr[] = `ls -sl`;
// Result: nurbsTorus52 //
```

Scripters will need to return the names of cameras in the scene. Since there is no limit to the number of viewports per file, the -ca flag queries for the shape nodes of the all renderable and non-renderable cameras. The default views are always called "front," "persp," "side," and "top," and these cannot be removed or renamed. Information on cameras will be discussed in subsequent chapters.

```
string $CamArr[] = `ls -ca`;
// Result: frontShape perspShape sideShape topShape //
```

Users can toggle between hidden and visible states of representation. To simplify modeling, this functionality lets unused or construction geometry to remain in the scene but not be rendered or clickable. To filter on only the visible in this scene (in this case, all objects are shown), use the -v flag.

```
string $VizArr[] = `ls -v`;
// Result: time1 renderPartition renderGlobalsList1 defaultLightList1 defaultShaderList1
postProcessList1 defaultRenderUtilityList1 lightList1 defaultTextureList1 lambert1
particleCloud1 initialShadingGroup initialParticleSE initialMaterialInfo shaderGlow1 dof1
defaultRenderGlobals defaultRenderQuality defaultResolution defaultLightSet
defaultObjectSet hardwareRenderGlobals characterPartition defaultHardwareRenderGlobals
ikSystem hyperGraphInfo hyperGraphLayout globalCacheControl dynController1 strokeGlobals
lightLinker1 layersFilter objectTypeFilter52 renderLayersFilter objectTypeFilter53
renderingSetsFilter objectTypeFilter54 relationshipPanel1LeftAttrFilter
relationshipPanel1RightAttrFilter layerManager defaultLayer renderLayerManager
defaultRenderLayer globalRender NS1 NS1Shape makeNurbSphere1 NS2 NS2Shape NS3 NS3Shape
NS4 NS4Shape NS5 NS5Shape NS6 NS6Shape NS7 NS7Shape NS8 NS8Shape NS9 NS9Shape NS10
NS10Shape NS11 NS11Shape NS12 NS12Shape NS13 NS13Shape NS14 NS14Shape NS15 NS15Shape NS16
NS16Shape NS17 NS17Shape NS18 NS18Shape NS19 NS19Shape NS20 NS20Shape NS21 NS21Shape NS22
NS22Shape NS23 NS23Shape NS24 NS24Shape NS25 NS25Shape NS26 NS26Shape NS27 NS27Shape NS28
NS28Shape NS29 NS29Shape NS30 NS30Shape NS31 NS31Shape NS32 NS32Shape NS33 NS33Shape NS34
NS34Shape NS35 NS35Shape NS36 NS36Shape NS37 NS37Shape NS38 NS38Shape NS39 NS39Shape NS40
NS40Shape NS41 NS41Shape NS42 NS42Shape NS43 NS43Shape NS44 NS44Shape NS45 NS45Shape NS46
NS46Shape NS47 NS47Shape NS48 NS48Shape NS49 NS49Shape NS50 NS50Shape NS51 NS51Shape NS52
NS52Shape NS53 NS53Shape NS54 NS54Shape NS55 NS55Shape NS56 NS56Shape NS57 NS57Shape NS58
NS58Shape NS59 NS59Shape NS60 NS60Shape nurbsTorus1 nurbsTorusShape1 makeNurbTorus1
nurbsTorus2 nurbsTorusShape2 makeNurbTorus2 nurbsTorus3 nurbsTorusShape3 makeNurbTorus3
nurbsTorus4 nurbsTorusShape4 makeNurbTorus4 nurbsTorus5 nurbsTorusShape5 makeNurbTorus5
nurbsTorus6 nurbsTorusShape6 makeNurbTorus6 nurbsTorus7 nurbsTorusShape7 makeNurbTorus7
nurbsTorus8 nurbsTorusShape8 makeNurbTorus8 nurbsTorus9 nurbsTorusShape9 makeNurbTorus9
nurbsTorus10 nurbsTorusShape10 makeNurbTorus10 nurbsTorus11 nurbsTorusShape11
makeNurbTorus11 nurbsTorus12 nurbsTorusShape12 makeNurbTorus12 nurbsTorus13
nurbsTorusShape13 makeNurbTorus13 nurbsTorus14 nurbsTorusShape14 makeNurbTorus14
nurbsTorus15 nurbsTorusShape15 makeNurbTorus15 nurbsTorus16 nurbsTorusShape16
```

```
makeNurbTorus16 nurbsTorus17 nurbsTorusShape17 makeNurbTorus17 nurbsTorus18
nurbsTorusShape18 makeNurbTorus18 nurbsTorusShape19 makeNurbTorus19
nurbsTorus20 nurbsTorusShape20 makeNurbTorus20 nurbsTorus21 nurbsTorusShape21
makeNurbTorus21 nurbsTorus22 nurbsTorusShape22 makeNurbTorus22 nurbsTorus23
nurbsTorusShape23 makeNurbTorus23 nurbsTorus24 nurbsTorusShape24 makeNurbTorus24
nurbsTorus25 nurbsTorusShape25 makeNurbTorus25 nurbsTorus26 nurbsTorusShape26
makeNurbTorus26 nurbsTorus27 nurbsTorusShape27 makeNurbTorus27 nurbsTorus28
nurbsTorusShape28 makeNurbTorus28 nurbsTorus29 nurbsTorusShape29 makeNurbTorus29
nurbsTorus30 nurbsTorusShape30 makeNurbTorus30 nurbsTorus31 nurbsTorusShape31
makeNurbTorus31 nurbsTorus32 nurbsTorusShape32 makeNurbTorus32 nurbsTorus33
nurbsTorusShape33 makeNurbTorus33 nurbsTorus34 nurbsTorusShape34 makeNurbTorus34
nurbsTorus35 nurbsTorusShape35 makeNurbTorus35 nurbsTorus36 nurbsTorusShape36
makeNurbTorus36 nurbsTorus37 nurbsTorusShape37 makeNurbTorus37 nurbsTorus38
nurbsTorusShape38 makeNurbTorus38 nurbsTorus39 nurbsTorusShape39 makeNurbTorus39
nurbsTorus40 nurbsTorusShape40 makeNurbTorus40 nurbsTorus41 nurbsTorusShape41
makeNurbTorus41 nurbsTorus42 nurbsTorusShape42 makeNurbTorus42 nurbsTorus43
nurbsTorusShape43 makeNurbTorus43 nurbsTorus44 nurbsTorusShape44 makeNurbTorus44
nurbsTorus45 nurbsTorusShape45 makeNurbTorus45 nurbsTorus46 nurbsTorusShape46
makeNurbTorus46 nurbsTorus47 nurbsTorusShape47 makeNurbTorus47 nurbsTorus48
nurbsTorusShape48 makeNurbTorus48 nurbsTorus49 nurbsTorusShape49 makeNurbTorus49
nurbsTorus50 nurbsTorusShape50 makeNurbTorus50 nurbsTorus51 nurbsTorusShape51
makeNurbTorus51 nurbsTorus52 nurbsTorusShape52 makeNurbTorus52 //
```

The second most important list flag behind the selection is the transform node name flag, shortened to -tr. All of the primitive's translate, rotate, scale and visibility data is stored under this node, so transform data is extremely crucial. Objects called Shape Nodes, which will be discussed later this chapter, should not be misconstrued as Transform Nodes. A common misconception about transform data is that the Geometry flag (-g) can provide the same string arrays, but it will return shape objects instead.

```
string $TrArr[] = `ls -tr`;
// Result: NS1 NS2 NS3 NS4 NS5 NS6 NS7 NS8 NS9 NS10 NS11 NS12 NS13 NS14 NS15 NS16 NS17
NS18 NS19 NS20 NS21 NS22 NS23 NS24 NS25 NS26 NS27 NS28 NS29 NS30 NS31 NS32 NS33 NS34 NS35
NS36 NS37 NS38 NS39 NS40 NS41 NS42 NS43 NS44 NS45 NS46 NS47 NS48 NS49 NS50 NS51 NS52 NS53
NS54 NS55 NS56 NS57 NS58 NS59 NS60 front nurbsTorus1 nurbsTorus2 nurbsTorus3 nurbsTorus4
nurbsTorus5 nurbsTorus6 nurbsTorus7 nurbsTorus8 nurbsTorus9 nurbsTorus10 nurbsTorus11
nurbsTorus12 nurbsTorus13 nurbsTorus14 nurbsTorus15 nurbsTorus16 nurbsTorus17
nurbsTorus18 nurbsTorus19 nurbsTorus20 nurbsTorus21 nurbsTorus22 nurbsTorus23
nurbsTorus24 nurbsTorus25 nurbsTorus26 nurbsTorus27 nurbsTorus28 nurbsTorus29
nurbsTorus30 nurbsTorus31 nurbsTorus32 nurbsTorus33 nurbsTorus34 nurbsTorus35
nurbsTorus36 nurbsTorus37 nurbsTorus38 nurbsTorus39 nurbsTorus40 nurbsTorus41
nurbsTorus42 nurbsTorus43 nurbsTorus44 nurbsTorus45 nurbsTorus46 nurbsTorus47
nurbsTorus48 nurbsTorus49 nurbsTorus50 nurbsTorus51 nurbsTorus52 persp side top //
```

Combining Flag for Lists

At first glance, the "ls" command appears to list all of the primitives generated from Code 9A. However, this will return all objects with transform data, like cameras at the bottom of the array. It is important to narrow or expand lists to obtain the desired content, for extra objects like cameras may negatively impact the codes reading them and cause errors. If one flag does not complete this task, combining them and using text strings can reduce the array.[§]

```
string $HArr[] = `ls -tr -ca`;
// Result: NS1 NS2 NS3 NS4 NS5 NS6 NS7 NS8 NS9 NS10 NS11 NS12 NS13 NS14 NS15 NS16 NS17
NS18 NS19 NS20 NS21 NS22 NS23 NS24 NS25 NS26 NS27 NS28 NS29 NS30 NS31 NS32 NS33 NS34 NS35
NS36 NS37 NS38 NS39 NS40 NS41 NS42 NS43 NS44 NS45 NS46 NS47 NS48 NS49 NS50 NS51 NS52 NS53
NS54 NS55 NS56 NS57 NS58 NS59 NS60 front nurbsTorus1 nurbsTorus2 nurbsTorus3 nurbsTorus4
nurbsTorus5 nurbsTorus6 nurbsTorus7 nurbsTorus8 nurbsTorus9 nurbsTorus10 nurbsTorus11
```

[§] MEL exhibits strange behavior with flag combinations which tend to not advertise if the filtration will Boolean intersect or union the list arrays. Much like "and" or "or" gates, combining flags may add to a list or only select objects that satisfy both conditions. Selection and Visibility flags intersect, while others usually union; test each combination prior to compiling

```
nurbsTorus12 nurbsTorus13 nurbsTorus14 nurbsTorus15 nurbsTorus16 nurbsTorus17
nurbsTorus18 nurbsTorus19 nurbsTorus20 nurbsTorus21 nurbsTorus22 nurbsTorus23
nurbsTorus24 nurbsTorus25 nurbsTorus26 nurbsTorus27 nurbsTorus28 nurbsTorus29
nurbsTorus30 nurbsTorus31 nurbsTorus32 nurbsTorus33 nurbsTorus34 nurbsTorus35
nurbsTorus36 nurbsTorus37 nurbsTorus38 nurbsTorus39 nurbsTorus40 nurbsTorus41
nurbsTorus42 nurbsTorus43 nurbsTorus44 nurbsTorus45 nurbsTorus46 nurbsTorus47
nurbsTorus48 nurbsTorus49 nurbsTorus50 nurbsTorus51 nurbsTorus52 persp side top
frontShape perspShape sideShape topShape //
```

string $HArr[] = `ls -v -tr -ca`;
```
// Result: NS1 NS2 NS3 NS4 NS5 NS6 NS7 NS8 NS9 NS10 NS11 NS12 NS13 NS14 NS15 NS16 NS17
NS18 NS19 NS20 NS21 NS22 NS23 NS24 NS25 NS26 NS27 NS28 NS29 NS30 NS31 NS32 NS33 NS34 NS35
NS36 NS37 NS38 NS39 NS40 NS41 NS42 NS43 NS44 NS45 NS46 NS47 NS48 NS49 NS50 NS51 NS52 NS53
NS54 NS55 NS56 NS57 NS58 NS59 NS60 nurbsTorus1 nurbsTorus2 nurbsTorus3 nurbsTorus4
nurbsTorus5 nurbsTorus6 nurbsTorus7 nurbsTorus8 nurbsTorus9 nurbsTorus10 nurbsTorus11
nurbsTorus12 nurbsTorus13 nurbsTorus14 nurbsTorus15 nurbsTorus16 nurbsTorus17
nurbsTorus18 nurbsTorus19 nurbsTorus20 nurbsTorus21 nurbsTorus22 nurbsTorus23
nurbsTorus24 nurbsTorus25 nurbsTorus26 nurbsTorus27 nurbsTorus28 nurbsTorus29
nurbsTorus30 nurbsTorus31 nurbsTorus32 nurbsTorus33 nurbsTorus34 nurbsTorus35
nurbsTorus36 nurbsTorus37 nurbsTorus38 nurbsTorus39 nurbsTorus40 nurbsTorus41
nurbsTorus42 nurbsTorus43 nurbsTorus44 nurbsTorus45 nurbsTorus46 nurbsTorus47
nurbsTorus48 nurbsTorus49 nurbsTorus50 nurbsTorus51 nurbsTorus52 //
```

Combining strings is generally more accurate and provides several avenues for effects authoring. The use of the wildcard character, the asterisk, lets matching portions of strings supplement the Boolean intersection of arrays.

string $N1Arr[] = `ls -tr "NS*"`;
```
// Result: NS1 NS2 NS3 NS4 NS5 NS6 NS7 NS8 NS9 NS10 NS11 NS12 NS13 NS14 NS15 NS16 NS17
NS18 NS19 NS20 NS21 NS22 NS23 NS24 NS25 NS26 NS27 NS28 NS29 NS30 NS31 NS32 NS33 NS34 NS35
NS36 NS37 NS38 NS39 NS40 NS41 NS42 NS43 NS44 NS45 NS46 NS47 NS48 NS49 NS50 NS51 NS52 NS53
NS54 NS55 NS56 NS57 NS58 NS59 NS60 //
```

string $N2Arr[] = `ls -tr "nurbsTorus*"`;
```
// Result: nurbsTorus1 nurbsTorus2 nurbsTorus3 nurbsTorus4 nurbsTorus5 nurbsTorus6
nurbsTorus7 nurbsTorus8 nurbsTorus9 nurbsTorus10 nurbsTorus11 nurbsTorus12 nurbsTorus13
nurbsTorus14 nurbsTorus15 nurbsTorus16 nurbsTorus17 nurbsTorus18 nurbsTorus19
nurbsTorus20 nurbsTorus21 nurbsTorus22 nurbsTorus23 nurbsTorus24 nurbsTorus25
nurbsTorus26 nurbsTorus27 nurbsTorus28 nurbsTorus29 nurbsTorus30 nurbsTorus31
nurbsTorus32 nurbsTorus33 nurbsTorus34 nurbsTorus35 nurbsTorus36 nurbsTorus37
nurbsTorus38 nurbsTorus39 nurbsTorus40 nurbsTorus41 nurbsTorus42 nurbsTorus43
nurbsTorus44 nurbsTorus45 nurbsTorus46 nurbsTorus47 nurbsTorus48 nurbsTorus49
nurbsTorus50 nurbsTorus51 nurbsTorus52 //
```

Listing Attributes

As stated before, attributes are the characteristics of objects. Depending upon the type of object or primitive, this list of characteristics changes. Some attributes are shared by all objects, while some are unique. To assess an object's specific list, the command "listAttr" should be utilized.

listAttr "NS1";
```
// Result: message caching isHistoricallyInteresting nodeState boundingBox boundingBoxMin
boundingBoxMinX boundingBoxMinY boundingBoxMinZ boundingBoxMax boundingBoxMaxX
boundingBoxMaxY boundingBoxMaxZ boundingBoxSize boundingBoxSizeX boundingBoxSizeY
boundingBoxSizeZ center boundingBoxCenterX boundingBoxCenterY boundingBoxCenterZ matrix
inverseMatrix worldMatrix worldInverseMatrix parentMatrix parentInverseMatrix visibility
intermediateObject template ghosting instObjGroups instObjGroups.objectGroups
instObjGroups.objectGroups.objectGrpCompList instObjGroups.objectGroups.objectGroupId
instObjGroups.objectGroups.objectGrpColor useObjectColor objectColor drawOverride
overrideDisplayType overrideLevelOfDetail overrideShading overrideTexturing
overridePlayback overrideEnabled overrideVisibility overrideColor lodVisibility
renderInfo identification layerRenderable layerOverrideColor ghostingControl
ghostCustomSteps ghostPreSteps ghostPostSteps ghostStepSize ghostFrames ghostRangeStart
ghostRangeEnd ghostDriver translate translateX translateY translateZ rotate rotateX
rotateY rotateZ rotateOrder scale scaleX scaleY scaleZ shear shearXY shearXZ shearYZ
rotatePivot rotatePivotX rotatePivotY rotatePivotZ rotatePivotTranslate
rotatePivotTranslateX rotatePivotTranslateY rotatePivotTranslateZ scalePivot scalePivotX
scalePivotY scalePivotZ scalePivotTranslate scalePivotTranslateX scalePivotTranslateY
scalePivotTranslateZ rotateAxis rotateAxisX rotateAxisY rotateAxisZ transMinusRotatePivot
```

```
transMinusRotatePivotX transMinusRotatePivotY transMinusRotatePivotZ minTransLimit
minTransXLimit minTransYLimit minTransZLimit maxTransLimit maxTransXLimit maxTransYLimit
maxTransZLimit minTransLimitEnable minTransXLimitEnable minTransYLimitEnable
minTransZLimitEnable maxTransLimitEnable maxTransXLimitEnable maxTransYLimitEnable
maxTransZLimitEnable minRotLimit minRotXLimit minRotYLimit minRotZLimit maxRotLimit
maxRotXLimit maxRotYLimit maxRotZLimit minRotLimitEnable minRotXLimitEnable
minRotYLimitEnable minRotZLimitEnable maxRotLimitEnable maxRotXLimitEnable
maxRotYLimitEnable maxRotZLimitEnable minScaleLimit minScaleXLimit minScaleYLimit
minScaleZLimit maxScaleLimit maxScaleXLimit maxScaleYLimit maxScaleZLimit
minScaleLimitEnable minScaleXLimitEnable minScaleYLimitEnable minScaleZLimitEnable
maxScaleLimitEnable maxScaleXLimitEnable maxScaleYLimitEnable maxScaleZLimitEnable
geometry xformMatrix selectHandle selectHandleX selectHandleY selectHandleZ
inheritsTransform displayHandle displayScalePivot displayRotatePivot displayLocalAxis
dynamics showManipDefault specifiedManipLocation rotateQuaternion rotateQuaternionX
rotateQuaternionY rotateQuaternionZ rotateQuaternionW rotationInterpolation //
```

These lists are generally used for attribute confirmation or identification, but occasionally programmers can integrate them into the script. This only occurs when the desired object list can contain disparate primitive types. The listed attributes can be stored into a string array and extracted by common indices.

```
string $NS1Attrs[] = `listAttr "NS1"`;
print $NS1Attrs[62];
```
Result: *"translateX" is printed. This attribute happens to be the 62nd attribute from the list generated by object "NS1."*

Other pertinent indexed attributes are as follows (differing primitive geometry types may be +/- 1 of the index value):

```
print $NS1Attrs[4];
boundingBox
print $NS1Attrs[17];
center
print $NS1Attrs[27];
visibility
print $NS1Attrs[61];
translate
print $NS1Attrs[62];
translateX
print $NS1Attrs[63];
translateY
print $NS1Attrs[64];
translateZ
print $NS1Attrs[65];
rotate
print $NS1Attrs[66];
rotateX
print $NS1Attrs[67];
rotateY
print $NS1Attrs[68];
rotateZ
print $NS1Attrs[70];
scale
print $NS1Attrs[71];
scaleX
print $NS1Attrs[72];
scaleY
print $NS1Attrs[73];
scaleZ
```

Attribute Sorting

Listed attribute string arrays can be lengthy and appear randomly organized. This proves difficult to survey for attribute verification, but by using the array command "sort," one can solve this issue. The example below is designed for visual verification, and this should not be used for indexed extraction as described earlier in this section.**

```
sort `listAttr NS1`;
// Result: boundingBox boundingBoxCenterX boundingBoxCenterY boundingBoxCenterZ
boundingBoxMax boundingBoxMaxX boundingBoxMaxY boundingBoxMaxZ boundingBoxMin
boundingBoxMinX boundingBoxMinY boundingBoxMinZ boundingBoxSize boundingBoxSizeX
boundingBoxSizeY boundingBoxSizeZ caching center displayHandle displayLocalAxis
displayRotatePivot displayScalePivot drawOverride dynamics geometry ghostCustomSteps
ghostDriver ghostFrames ghostPostSteps ghostPreSteps ghostRangeEnd ghostRangeStart
ghostStepSize ghosting ghostingControl identification inheritsTransform instObjGroups
instObjGroups.objectGroups instObjGroups.objectGroups.objectGroupId
instObjGroups.objectGroups.objectGrpColor instObjGroups.objectGroups.objectGrpCompList
intermediateObject inverseMatrix isHistoricallyInteresting layerOverrideColor
layerRenderable lodVisibility matrix maxRotLimit maxRotLimitEnable maxRotXLimit
maxRotXLimitEnable maxRotYLimit maxRotYLimitEnable maxRotZLimit maxRotZLimitEnable
maxScaleLimit maxScaleLimitEnable maxScaleXLimit maxScaleXLimitEnable maxScaleYLimit
maxScaleYLimitEnable maxScaleZLimit maxScaleZLimitEnable maxTransLimit
maxTransLimitEnable maxTransXLimit maxTransXLimitEnable maxTransYLimit
maxTransYLimitEnable maxTransZLimit maxTransZLimitEnable message minRotLimit
minRotLimitEnable minRotXLimit minRotXLimitEnable minRotYLimit minRotYLimitEnable
minRotZLimit minRotZLimitEnable minScaleLimit minScaleLimitEnable minScaleXLimit
minScaleXLimitEnable minScaleYLimit minScaleYLimitEnable minScaleZLimit
minScaleZLimitEnable minTransLimit minTransLimitEnable minTransXLimit
minTransXLimitEnable minTransYLimit minTransYLimitEnable minTransZLimit
minTransZLimitEnable nodeState objectColor overrideColor overrideDisplayType
overrideEnabled overrideLevelOfDetail overridePlayback overrideShading overrideTexturing
overrideVisibility parentInverseMatrix parentMatrix renderInfo rotate rotateAxis
rotateAxisX rotateAxisY rotateAxisZ rotateOrder rotatePivot rotatePivotTranslate
rotatePivotTranslateX rotatePivotTranslateY rotatePivotTranslateZ rotatePivotX
rotatePivotY rotatePivotZ rotateQuaternion rotateQuaternionW rotateQuaternionX
rotateQuaternionY rotateQuaternionZ rotateX rotateY rotateZ rotationInterpolation scale
scalePivot scalePivotTranslate scalePivotTranslateX scalePivotTranslateY
scalePivotTranslateZ scalePivotX scalePivotY scalePivotZ scaleX scaleY scaleZ
selectHandle selectHandleX selectHandleY selectHandleZ shear shearXY shearXZ shearYZ
showManipDefault specifiedManipLocation template transMinusRotatePivot
transMinusRotatePivotX transMinusRotatePivotY transMinusRotatePivotZ translate translateX
translateY translateZ useObjectColor visibility worldInverseMatrix worldMatrix
xformMatrix //
```

Getting Singular Attributes

Similar to using the query flag in Chapter 5, "getting" attributes returns numerical or alphabetic data about an object. Attribute lists tend to be much more comprehensive than query flags, so this method is regarded as a best practice for existing object modification. This can be printed for visual verification or also stored into a float, integer or string variable.

There exist ten relevant attributes residing under the transform object that deal with a single value of modification. These characteristics have only one input.

```
visibility
translateX
```

** Technically, scripters can use the sorted attribute list. However, some primitives may have a different order of characteristics, which may place the alphabetic order of the main transform attributes in flux. If a loop was constructed with two different primitive types, like a torus and polysphere, then it is possible that the sorted array list may have "translateX" in a different index than the other. Verify primitive attribute list indices prior to compiling.

```
translateY
translateZ
rotateX
rotateY
rotateZ
scaleX
scaleY
scaleZ
```

When attempting to unlock the values behind a particular attribute, the object name should precede the attribute separated by a period. The command "getAttr" must be used to extract the data.

[Command]   +   [Object Name]   +   .   +   [Attribute Name]

For example…

getAttr NS6.rotateZ;
Result: *"603.175988" is printed.*

or

getAttr nurbsTorus12.visibility;
Result: *"1" is printed.*

In the case of the Z rotation, a float is returned. A singular attribute will usually return a real number, however a few variables, like visibility, act like switches. These return integers that are either 0 (off) or 1 (on). In the interface, these are considered checkboxes. When dealing with transformations, translate units are in centimeters (as defined in the settings and preferences), rotational values are in degrees and scalar attributes are set to real numbers.

The last two examples simply print the attribute and do little to store the data in a usable way.   To assign a singular attribute value to a variable, use the backticks and singular data-types.

float $rZ6 = `getAttr NS6.rotateZ`;
Result: *"603.175988" is printed and stored in the variable "$rZ6."*

or

int $Viz6 = `getAttr nurbsTorus12.visibility`;
Result: *"1" is printed and stored in the integer variable "$Viz6."*

Getting Array Attributes
There exist six relevant attributes residing under the transform object that deal with a multiple values of modification. These characteristics have three or more inputs.

```
boundingBoxMin
boundingBoxMax
center
translate
rotate
scale
```

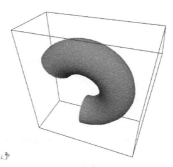

The bounding box is an invisible, representational rectangular solid encapsulating the queried object. This read-only data is extremely useful for proximity calculations and other advanced topics. Simply put, the "min" pertains to the left-most, bottom-most, back-most XYZ coordinate from this invisible box. The "max" deals with the right-most, top-most, front-most XYZ coordinate. These two points give a crude indication of the extents of the geometry by implying a three-dimensional hypotenuse. The "center" attribute is in most cases, but not always, the centroid of this bounding box.

Similar to singular attribute retrieval, the object name should precede the attribute separated by a period. The command "getAttr" must be used to extract the data. The only discernable difference will appear in the result; more than one value will be printed.

   [Command] + [Object Name] + . + [Attribute Name]

For example…

getAttr nurbsTorus12.boundingBoxMin;
Result: *"10.25 -3.824408 3.25" is printed.*

or

getAttr NS6.rotate;
Result: *"13.298718 -3.851321 603.175988" is printed.*

As with singular values, translations, rotations and scales are in units of centimeters, degrees and real numbers, respectively. Instead of dedicating an attribute name to each of the X or Y or Z coordinates of its transform matrix, multi-value attributes coalesce all three values into one. The last two examples just print the attribute and do little to store the data in a usable way. To assign a multiple attribute value to a variable, use the backticks and array data-types.

float $VB12[] = `getAttr nurbsTorus12.boundingBoxMin`;
Result: *"10.25 -3.824408 3.25" is printed and stored in the array "$VB12."*

or

```
float $r6[] = `getAttr NS6.rotate`;
```
Result: *"13.298718 -3.851321 603.175988" is printed and stored in the array "$r6."*

To punctuate these sections, it should be explained that the variable storing an attribute's information is NOT connected to the attribute value. This process of getting attributes just takes a snapshot of its current placement and holds onto that number or numbers. If the rotation of the object "NS6" changes in the future, the variable "$r6" would remain at "13.298718 -3.851321 603.175988." If the scripter re-queried the rotate attribute later, it would return the new orientation. (Connecting attributes can be accomplished via the "connectAttr" command, but this topic will not be covered in this edition.)

Working with getAttr
Most singular attributes are an element in a multiple attribute. This introduces a good deal of redundancy in the large attribute list, and scripters should use the array attributes to query values most often. The lines below are recorded from the History Window and show all of the relevant attributes.

```
int $Viz6 = `getAttr NS6.visibility`;
// Result: 1 //
float $tX6 = `getAttr NS6.translateX`;
// Result: 10 //
float $tY6 = `getAttr NS6.translateY`;
// Result: 10 //
float $tZ6 = `getAttr NS6.translateZ`;
// Result: 3.5 //
float $rX6 = `getAttr NS6.rotateX`;
// Result: 13.298718 //
float $rY6 = `getAttr NS6.rotateY`;
// Result: -3.851321 //
float $rZ6 = `getAttr NS6.rotateZ`;
// Result: 603.175988 //
float $sX6 = `getAttr NS6.scaleX`;
// Result: 1 //
float $sY6 = `getAttr NS6.scaleY`;
// Result: 1 //
float $sZ6 = `getAttr NS6.scaleZ`;
// Result: 1 //
float $VB12[] = `getAttr nurbsTorus12.boundingBoxMin`;
// Result: 10.25 -3.824408 3.25 //
float $VB12[] = `getAttr nurbsTorus12.boundingBoxMax`;
// Result: 11.75 -0.254243 6.798116 //
float $VC12[] = `getAttr nurbsTorus12.center`;
// Result: 11 -2.039325 5.024058 //
float $t12[] = `getAttr nurbsTorus12.translate`;
// Result: 0 0 0 //
float $t6[] = `getAttr NS6.translate`;
// Result: 10 10 3.5 //
float $r6[] = `getAttr NS6.rotate`;
// Result: 13.298718 -3.851321 603.175988 //
float $s6[] = `getAttr NS6.scale`;
// Result: 1 1 1 //
```

When reducing this list to just the transform data, these nine lines return each number as separate variables. This practice is cumbersome, but produces accurate results.

```
float $tX6 = `getAttr NS6.translateX`;
// Result: 10 //
float $tY6 = `getAttr NS6.translateY`;
// Result: 10 //
float $tZ6 = `getAttr NS6.translateZ`;
// Result: 3.5 //
float $rX6 = `getAttr NS6.rotateX`;
// Result: 13.298718 //
float $rY6 = `getAttr NS6.rotateY`;
// Result: -3.851321 //
float $rZ6 = `getAttr NS6.rotateZ`;
// Result: 603.175988 //
float $sX6 = `getAttr NS6.scaleX`;
// Result: 1 //
float $sY6 = `getAttr NS6.scaleY`;
// Result: 1 //
float $sZ6 = `getAttr NS6.scaleZ`;
// Result: 1 //
```

The more concise way of dealing with attributes is to use arrays as often as possible. The previous nine lines have been reduced to three. (With some linear algebra, the "matrix" attribute will reduce these lines to one.)

```
float $t6[] = `getAttr NS6.translate`;
// Result: 10 10 3.5 //
float $r6[] = `getAttr NS6.rotate`;
// Result: 13.298718 -3.851321 603.175988 //
float $s6[] = `getAttr NS6.scale`;
// Result: 1 1 1 //
```

As users make changes to the movement, rotation, and scale of the objects in the scene, these attributes update in real time. The next series of codes are minor manipulations of objects by the "move" command. Immediately, the translate attribute is recorded. The original translate location of primitive "NS6" is X = 10, Y = 10 and Z = 3.5.

Move "NS6" 1.2 units in each positive axial direction…

```
move -r 1.2 1.2 1.2 NS6;
float $t6[] = `getAttr NS6.translate`;
// Result: 11.2 11.2 4.7 //
```

Move "NS6" 1.2 units in the positive Z direction…

```
move -r 0 0 1.2 NS6;
float $t6[] = `getAttr NS6.translate`;
// Result: 11.2 11.2 5.9 //
```

Move "NS6" 1.2 units in the positive Z direction again…

```
move -r 0 0 1.2 NS6;
float $t6[] = `getAttr NS6.translate`;
// Result: 11.2 11.2 7.1 //
```

Move "NS6" to the world space location of (0, 0, 1.2)…

```
move -ws 0 0 1.2 NS6;
float $t6[] = `getAttr NS6.translate`;
// Result: 0 0 1.2 //
```

When the script moves the object, the world space location of the translate is returned. The world space location of objects becomes extremely important for proximity calculations as well, however, this should not be taken for granted as the centroid or even close to the object. Later chapters will reveal more accurate ways of determining the location of an object. A telltale identifier of inaccurate location values is if pivot flags were utilized in the creation of the primitive. This is why it is advised to never or limitedly use flags in this manner. For example, examine the results from object "nurbsTorus12," which had utilized pivot flags in Code 9A.

```
float $VB12[] = `getAttr nurbsTorus12.boundingBoxMin`;
// Result: 10.25 -3.824408 3.25 //
float $VB12[] = `getAttr nurbsTorus12.boundingBoxMax`;
// Result: 11.75 -0.254243 6.798116 //
float $VC12[] = `getAttr nurbsTorus12.center`;
// Result: 11 -2.039325 5.024058 //
float $t12[] = `getAttr nurbsTorus12.translate`;
// Result: 0 0 0 //
```

In this scenario, the bounding box and center are clearly far from the origin of the scene. Paradoxically, the translate location, which is often regarded as the world space location of the object, is returning (0, 0, 0). Both cannot be correct, and after visual confirmation of the scene, the translate attribute is misleading[††].

Setting Singular Attributes
All attributes are readable; this is the concept of "getting" data and has been detailed in the previous sections. The next logical extension of this process is to introduce the capability to write data to attributes. This is called "setting" and is accomplished by the command "setAttr." Not all values are writable, and attempts to change these will prompt coders with "read-only" messages.

[††] In a technical sense, the translate is not expressing incorrect data, for no "move" operation has occurred on the primitive. Since the translate attribute always returns the latest calculation of the world space location of the sequence of "move" operations, this is the correct value, because this is the zeroth "move" operation, it resides at the origin.

Identical to the "getAttr" command, there exist ten relevant attributes residing under the transform object that dealing a single value of alteration. These characteristics have only one input.

```
visibility
translateX
translateY
translateZ
rotateX
rotateY
rotateZ
scaleX
scaleY
scaleZ
```

When attempting to reset the values behind a particular attribute, the object name should precede the attribute separated by a period. The command "setAttr" must be used to apply the data and end with the desired value.

[Command] + [Object Name] + . + [Attribute Name] [Value]

For example...

setAttr NS6.rotateZ -30;
Result: *The object "NS6" has been rotated to the world space orientation of -30 degrees.*

When working with checkbox or Boolean attributes, the string "on" is identical to 1 and "off" corresponds to 0. These strings are not returned when using "getAttr," but will function in this case.

setAttr NS6.visibility off;
setAttr NS6.visibility on;
setAttr NS6.visibility 0;
setAttr NS6.visibility 1;
Result: *The object "NS6" has been hidden and shown twice.*

Setting Array Attributes
There exist three relevant attributes residing under the transform object that deal with a multiple values of alteration. These characteristics have a unique means of modification.

```
translate
rotate
scale
```

When attempting to reset the values behind a particular attribute, the object name should precede the attribute separated by a period. The command "setAttr" must be used to apply the data and end with the desired type and value.

[Command] + [Object Name] + . + [Attribute Name] [Type] [Value]

For example…

```
setAttr NS6.rotate -type "double3" 90 0 -30;
```
Result: *The object "NS6" has been rotated to the world space orientation of (90, 0, -30) degrees.*

The flag "-type" prepares the command for a multi-value data-type. There are several appropriate strings that can follow this flag and each can be found in the command reference. The most common type string is the "double3," which sets real number attributes in groups of three, the standard for XYZ or RGB coordinates. Singular string types should have the word "string" which format naming attributes.

All transform characteristics are shown below to demonstrate translation, rotation and scaling. With the exception of relative modifications, these methods can replace basic transformation commands "move," "rotate," and "scale." The use of "setAttr" is an improvement on two fronts: selection is ignored (decreasing memory usage) and the number of lines of code is reduced.

```
setAttr NS6.translateX 5.25;
setAttr NS6.translateY -6.25;
setAttr NS6.translateZ 2.33;
setAttr NS6.rotateX 90;
setAttr NS6.rotateY 0;
setAttr NS6.rotateZ -30;
setAttr NS6.scaleX 1.23;
setAttr NS6.scaleY 1.23;
setAttr NS6.scaleZ 1.23;
```

These can be reduced to three lines by utilizing the multiple value configuration…

```
setAttr NS6.translate -type "double3" 5.25 -6.25 2.33;
setAttr NS6.rotate -type "double3" 90 0 -30;
setAttr NS6.scale -type "double3" 1.23 1.23 1.23;
```

getAttr and setAttr with Variables
Attributes can be concatenated with variables in two ways: the value and the name. Utilizing variables to set the attribute can be an advanced way of managing complex formal relationships. When scripters alter the value of an attribute or concatenate the name of the object with variables, it eliminates the need of hard-coding the identity of objects. The benefit of this is the ability to place these retrieval commands inside of a loop and batch test the attributes of a collection of geometry.

In the previous examples in this chapter, value change has been limited to fixed, static numbers. With all static inputs in programming, these can be replaced with dynamic variables, as long as the data-types match. For example…

```
float $xR6 = 90;
setAttr NS6.rotateX $xR6;
```

or

```
float $xR6 = 90;
float $yR6 = 0;
float $zR6 = -30;
setAttr NS6.rotate -type "double3" $xR6 $yR6 $zR6;
```

or

```
float $RArr6[2] = {90, 0, -30};
setAttr NS6.rotate -type "double3" $RArr6[0] $RArr6[1] $RArr6[2];
```

//Hard-Coding:
/* When programmers use static values in the process of authoring a script, this is referred to as "hard-coding." An advantage to hard-coding is that users cannot make changes to crucial data. For example, if a script was designed to convert units, the author should not expose the values for conversion for users may accidentally change 25.4 to 0.3937, and get incorrect results. However, hard-coding presents several disadvantages, namely the script may not accommodate for all geometric cases. An example of this is not to use variables in the retrieval of attributes. If concatenation is the only tool for batch attribute querying, then the user must preload all transform names with a perfect naming convention, a process extremely susceptible to human error. A balance of portability and hard-coding is necessary for all scripts. */

getAttr and setAttr with Variables and Concatenation

Setting the values of singular and plural is simple, but altering the characters of the attribute name string is slightly more complex. Using concatenation, this process opens several avenues for multiple variation. In the following examples, this manual will reveal how to extract attributes from geometry names stored in a variable. This will expand the ability to calculate and store data from a list or unknown objects.

Concatenation must be used to construct the variable names. As with the previouse examples, all object and attribute names are explicitly typed following the "getAttr" and "setAttr" commands. These names can be replaced with variables or concatenated strings encapsulated with parentheses. More on concatenation can be found in Chapter 4.

When a name ("NS7") is stored in a singular string variable ("$CurName"), the variable name cannot be adjoined to the attribute name ("$CurName.rotate"). This is a common misconception about MEL scripting and it is poor practice[‡‡].

```
//Incorrect Code.  Errors will result.//
string $CurName = "NS7";
```

[‡‡] Sometimes this pseudo-concatenation of variables and partial strings can return the correct name-attribute, but it is randomly reproducible. Full concatenation using the techniques described later in this chapter and section are best practice.

```
float $CurRot[] = `getAttr $CurName.rotate`;
//Incorrect Code.  Errors will result.//
```

The correct way to return the name is to use an enclosed string or calculated string adjacent to the command. The attribute name must be surrounded by quotes along with the period. Because the quoted attribute (`".rotate"`) and variable (`"$CurName"`) are encapsulated by parentheses (`"($CurName+".rotate")"`), the arithmetic calculation occurs prior to the execution of the attribute command, appearing as the completed name-attribute (`"NS7.rotate"`) string to the application.

```
string $CurName = "NS7";
float $CurRot[] = `getAttr ($CurName+".rotate")`;
```
Result: *The rotations from object "NS7" are printed. (-0.124432, 0.512224, 723.692056)*

This procedure works for array values, for in most cases, there will not be a dedicated variable for the name of objects. Most will come from lists. This example determines the rotations for the seventh object in the list of all "NS" transforms.

```
string $NSArr[] = `ls -tr "NS*"`;
float $CurRot[] = `getAttr ($NSArr[6]+".rotate")`;
```
Result: *The rotations from object "NS7" are printed. (-0.124432, 0.512224, 723.692056)*

The same can be applied to setting attributes. As long as the concatenation is encapsulated by parentheses, the application will read the string as the name-attribute combination necessary for data revision and extraction.

```
string $NSArr[] = `ls -tr "NS*"`;
setAttr ($NSArr[6]+".rotateY") 95;
```
Result: *The Y-axis rotation from object "NS7" is changed to 95 degrees.*

```
string $NSArr[] = `ls -tr "NS*"`;
setAttr ($NSArr[6]+".rotate") -type "double3" -30 95 110;
```
Result: *The rotations from object "NS7" are changed to (-30, 95, 110) degrees.*

As with all arrays, the index can be replaced with a dynamic variable as well. In the next example, the counter (`"$U_8"`) takes the place of the list array index. This allows for a loop to cycle through the first twenty-five objects in the list array (`"$NSArr[]"`). This sample code also reinterprets the data and constructs a clean list of coordinates based on the translate attribute.

```
string $NSArr[] = `ls -tr "NS*"`;
int $U_8 = 0;
do {
        float $CurXYZ[] = `getAttr ($NSArr[$U_8]+".translate")`;
        print ("("+$CurXYZ[0]+","+$CurXYZ[1]+","+$CurXYZ[2]+")\n");
```

```
    currentTime $U_8;
    $U_8++;
} while ($U_8 < 25);
```

Result:
```
(0,0,0)
(0,2,0.7)
(1,4,1.4)
(3,6,2.1)
(6,8,2.8)
(10,10,3.5)
(15,12,4.2)
(21,14,4.9)
(28,16,5.6)
(36,18,6.3)
(45,20,7)
(55,22,7.7)
(66,24,8.4)
(78,26,9.1)
(91,28,9.8)
(105,30,10.5)
(120,32,11.2)
(136,34,11.9)
(153,36,12.6)
(171,38,13.3)
(190,40,14)
(210,42,14.7)
(231,44,15.4)
(253,46,16.1)
(276,48,16.8)
// Result: 24 //
```

Variable indices are available for setting attributes also. In this example, the ninth through fifteenth objects in the list array are moved to the world space location of (5, 9.3, 0).

```
string $NSArr[] = `ls -tr "NS*"`;
int $i = 10;
do {
    setAttr ($NSArr[$i]+".translate") -type "double3" 5 9.3 0;
    currentTime $i;
    $i++;
} while ($i < 16);
```
Result: *Items NS10-NS16 are moved to the world space location of (5, 9.3, 0).*

Diverse variation can be achieved by combining all of the concatenation techniques and variable replacements from the last section. This is a standard-to-advanced mode of extracting and modifying attributes in this programming language, but ultimately affords the most potential for effects authoring. In the last example in this section, this name concatenation, variable indices, and static number replacement occurs.

```
string $NSArr[] = `ls -tr "NS*"`;
```

```
for ($k=1;$k<25;$k++) {
    for ($j=1;$j<5;$j++) {
        float $C4 = $k-$j;
        setAttr ($NSArr[$j]+".translate") -type "double3" $C4 $C4 $C4;
        currentTime $j;
    }
}
```

Result: *Items NS1-NS4 are moved in a simulated animated diagonal direction.*

Working with Nodes

For the majority of the chapter, this manual has explained only half of the information about objects. Knowing attributes are elements of nodes, it may appear strange to explain a part of the system before clarifying its hierarchy. However, most of the attributes dealt with in this chapter correspond to commands from earlier chapters, which all reside in the principle node, called the Transform Node. This node also manages the name of the object, so for the sake of continuity, these characteristics were placed at a higher priority.

Returning to the analogy of the dashboard, nodes appeared as different dashboard consoles and attributes are switches and gauges. Each console is designed for different tasks (like the radio, velocity and climate controls) and each have their own family of buttons and gauges. Nodes follow the same structure, generally in this order: Transform, Shape, Make, Shader Group and Shader Nodes. Most primitives tend to abide this order, with the exception of duplicated geometry. These nodes house the different attributes connected to queried geometry, and unlocking another node opens a treasure box of characteristics.

For the remainder of the chapter, we will be using the object "NS1" to display its node consoles. This will be the virtual guinea pig on which we will dissect.

Transform Nodes

The Transform Nodes contents have been covered in detail. This node is the default condition of any object, be it geometry, cameras, or other, and it corresponds to name of the object directly. When a modeler clicks on a sphere, "nurbsSphere1" is the Transform Node name, not the object name. Equally, when scripters type...

```
getAttr NS1.rotateZ
```

they are actually accessing the Transform Node named "NS1," not an object named "NS1." For the list of all Transform Node attributes, review the earlier sections in this chapter.

Shape Nodes

When examining the geometric composition of an object, users will find vertices and faces with polygons, isoparms and control vertices with NURBS, and modifier points with subdivision surfaces. These are universal to each respective geometry type, regardless of their primitive form. The Shape Node manages the attributes concerning the primitive's polygon/NURBS/Sub-D geometry.

The name of a Shape Node is often linked to the name of the Transform Node. When working with an object that was named at creation, the name of the Shape Node is just a combination of the Transform name and the characters "Shape." For object "NS1," the name of its corresponding Shape Node is...

```
NS1Shape
```

For objects without unique naming at creation, like default names ("nurbsTorus7"), this naming convention is not as simple. Shape Nodes for default name strings separate the Transform name and place the word "Shape" inside. The object "nurbsTorus7" has a Shape Node name of...

```
nurbsTorusShape7
```

For this reason, it is advised to always provide unique names for objects when creating or duplicating them. Concatenating the characters "Shape" into the middle of a Transform Node name can be cumbersome.

Just like Transform Node attributes, scripters can print the attributes of the Shape Node using the command "listAttr." Both the Transform and Shape share several attribute names, but ultimately, the latter tends to deal only with visualization and geometric values. Because some of these attributes are more representative rather than writable, they will in most cases only report the geometric characteristics of the form, rather than allow the coder to manipulate them.

```
listAttr NS1Shape;
// Result: message caching isHistoricallyInteresting nodeState boundingBox boundingBoxMin
boundingBoxMinX boundingBoxMinY boundingBoxMinZ boundingBoxMax boundingBoxMaxX
boundingBoxMaxY boundingBoxMaxZ boundingBoxSize boundingBoxSizeX boundingBoxSizeY
boundingBoxSizeZ center boundingBoxCenterX boundingBoxCenterY boundingBoxCenterZ matrix
inverseMatrix worldMatrix worldInverseMatrix parentMatrix parentInverseMatrix visibility
intermediateObject template ghosting instObjGroups instObjGroups.objectGroups
instObjGroups.objectGroups.objectGrpCompList instObjGroups.objectGroups.objectGroupId
instObjGroups.objectGroups.objectGrpColor useObjectColor objectColor drawOverride
overrideDisplayType overrideLevelOfDetail overrideShading overrideTexturing
overridePlayback overrideEnabled overrideVisibility overrideColor lodVisibility
renderInfo identification layerRenderable layerOverrideColor ghostingControl
ghostCustomSteps ghostPreSteps ghostPostSteps ghostStepSize ghostFrames ghostRangeStart
ghostRangeEnd ghostDriver renderType renderVolume visibleFraction motionBlur
visibleInReflections visibleInRefractions castsShadows receiveShadows
maxVisibilitySamplesOverride maxVisibilitySamples geometryAntialiasingOverride
antialiasingLevel shadingSamplesOverride shadingSamples maxShadingSamples
volumeSamplesOverride volumeSamples depthJitter ignoreSelfShadowing primaryVisibility
referenceObject compInstObjGroups compInstObjGroups.compObjectGroups
compInstObjGroups.compObjectGroups.compObjectGrpCompList
compInstObjGroups.compObjectGroups.compObjectGroupId tweak relativeTweak controlPoints
controlPoints.xValue controlPoints.yValue controlPoints.zValue weights tweakLocation
blindDataNodes uvSet uvSet.uvSetName uvSet.uvSetPoints uvSet.uvSetPoints.uvSetPointsU
uvSet.uvSetPoints.uvSetPointsV uvSet.uvSetTweakLocation currentUVSet doubleSided opposite
smoothShading boundingBoxScale boundingBoxScaleX boundingBoxScaleY boundingBoxScaleZ
featureDisplacement initialSampleRate extraSampleRate textureThreshold normalThreshold
displayHWEnvironment header create local worldSpace divisionsU divisionsV curvePrecision
curvePrecisionShaded simplifyMode simplifyU simplifyV smoothEdge smoothEdgeRatio
useChordHeight objSpaceChordHeight useChordHeightRatio edgeSwap useMinScreen selCVDisp
dispCV dispEP dispHull dispGeometry dispOrigin numberU modeU numberV modeV chordHeight
chordHeightRatio minScreen formU formV cached trimFace patchUVIds inPlace tweakSizeU
```

```
tweakSizeV minMaxRangeU minValueU maxValueU minMaxRangeV minValueV maxValueV degreeUV
degreeU degreeV spansUV spansU spansV displayRenderTessellation renderTriangleCount
fixTextureWarp gridDivisionPerSpanU gridDivisionPerSpanV explicitTessellationAttributes
uDivisionsFactor vDivisionsFactor curvatureTolerance basicTessellationType dispSF
normalsDisplayScale //
```

Some attributes are more ubiquitous than others. Below is a list of relevant characteristics, only found in the Shape Node:

```
motionBlur
visibleInReflections
visibleInRefractions
castsShadows
receiveShadows
spansU
spansV
spansUV
```

When retrieving and setting attributes from a Shape Node, the same syntax applies for all attributes. The commands "getAttr" and "setAttr" must be used in conjuction with "Shape" name-attribute. To get the values for the U and V isoparms…

```
getAttr NS1Shape.spansU;
// Result: 4 //
getAttr NS1Shape.spansV;
// Result: 8 //
getAttr NS1Shape.spansUV;
// Result: 4 8 //
```

To set the value of the motionBlur…

```
setAttr NS1Shape.motionBlur 0;
```

Make Nodes
The Make Node contains data for characteristics unique to the creation object form, like cylinders, spheres, cubes, planes, et cetera. NURBS, polygons and subdivision surfaces all have different primitive shape-types (see Chapter 6 for more information). Each of these forms, when created, generates a Make Node connected to the main object. This node only applies to primitives regardless if their geometry is modified, contorted, or unrecognizable; duplicated or datumized geometry will retain no Make Node.

The Make Node naming convention does not respect the given or default name. Regardless of the given name, the Make Node will automatically generate a name based on the latest instance of the node. Most Make Nodes appear to have the string "make" prefixing the name of the object, however, this is deceiving. For object "NS1," the Make Node name is…

```
makeNurbSphere1
```

When deconstructed, "makeNurbSphere1" is actually "make" + "NurbSphere1" where "NurbSphere1" is the first instance of any NURBS sphere in the scene and not the given name at creation ("NS1")[§§]. A poor practice would be to concatenate the Make Node name from the Transform name. For example, the Make Node name for the object "nurbsTorus37" is...

```
makeNurbTorus37
```

A common mistake is to assume the Transform name can be added to the end of "make." Upon closer inspection, "make" + "NurbTorus37" is extremely different than "make" + "nurbsTorus37," because of the case sensitivity and missing "s." Also, but not shown in this scene, the name of the Tranform count does not always directly correspond to the Make Node count. Concatenation cannot be used for identification, and other techniques that explain how to traverse the nodes of an object will be covered later in this chapter.

When listing the attributes of a Make Node, the list is substantially smaller than the Transform or Shape nodes. These attributes are specialized for the geometry type. Objects like spheres would have radii and sweeping angles, while cubes would focus on lengths, widths and heights.

Here is a list of a typical Make Node NURBS sphere...

```
listAttr makeNurbSphere1;
// Result: message caching isHistoricallyInteresting nodeState
pivot pivotX pivotY pivotZ axis axisX axisY axisZ outputSurface
radius startSweep endSweep useTolerance degree sections spans
tolerance heightRatio topCapCurve bottomCapCurve
absoluteSweepDifference //
```

Compared to the list of typical NURBS torus Make Node attributes...

```
listAttr makeNurbTorus37;
// Result: message caching isHistoricallyInteresting nodeState
pivot pivotX pivotY pivotZ axis axisX axisY axisZ outputSurface
radius startSweep endSweep useTolerance degree sections spans
tolerance heightRatio topCapCurve bottomCapCurve
absoluteSweepDifference minorSweep //
```

When they were created, the nurbsToruses in this scene (derived from Code 9A) have some attributes altered by simple mathematics. With the Make Node name, scripters can access and modify this data. As with all attributes, "setAttr" and "getAttr" are paramount.

```
getAttr makeNurbTorus37.endSweep;
```

[§§] In the "NS" object list, only the first object appears to have a Make Node. Only created geometry can preserve a Make Node, and all of the extra "spheres" are just duplicates. Even though duplicates are nearly identical in shape to a primitive, this distinction restricts its node count to just a Transform, Shape, Shader Group and Shader.

```
// Result: 666 //
setAttr makeNurbTorus37.endSweep 240;
```
Result: *The object "nurbsTorus37" has a new end sweep value of 240 degrees.*

Shader Group and Shader Nodes

The last area of geometric attributing is its representational qualities. In the field of animation, this pertains to the materials and colors assigned to an object or surface. Objects using the default initial material have a temporary node called the Initial Shader Group Node ("initialShadingGroup") and all objects have a material, called a Shader. Shaders will be covered more completely in a chapter devoted to rendering.

The default material in every scene is called "lambert1" and is always initially grey in tone. All objects enter the scene with this material until it is replaced with another by a modeler or code.

Traversing Nodes

Since concatenation is a limited or inadequate way of determining an objects node composition, scripters should use listing commands to return these names. The Transform, Shape, Make and Shader nodes are all connected, and there are a family of commands that can unlock these strings. Storing these arrays will increase the functionality of the code, because these words will not require hard-coding.

There are three listing commands (in addition to "listAttr") that manage associations: "listHistory," "listConnections," and "listRelatives." There is no command that simply prints associated nodes, because different objects can share several consoles. Traversing nodes can be a bit circuitous, but each step shifts across the spectrum of nodes.

To find the Shape and Make nodes of object "NS1"...

```
listHistory NS1;
// Result: NS1Shape makeNurbSphere1 //
```

Just listing the names will not be useful for coding, so users should store these strings in arrays. If the object does not have a Make Node, then this array will shorten by one string.

```
string $NS1H[] = `listHistory NS1`;
// Result: NS1Shape makeNurbSphere1 //
```

Using this array, coders can slide across the node list by using the command "listConnections." This will print the connected names to the Shape Node pulled from the Transform object's listed history. The Shape node is always the first object in the History for any primitive, which can be substituted by the zeroth member of the string array. Using this syntax repeatedly will shift across the spectrum and end up with the shader associated with that particular primitive.

```
string $NS1H[] = `listHistory NS1`;
// Result: NS1Shape makeNurbSphere1 //
string $NS1SG[] = `listConnections $NS1H[0]`;
// Result: initialShadingGroup makeNurbSphere1 //
string $NS1SH[] = `listConnections $NS1SG[0]`;
// Result: lambert1 lightLinker1 initialMaterialInfo
renderPartition ...//
```

By running the aforementioned code, scripters have stored all of the names associated with the Transform and Object name of "NS1." This can be applied to all objects and these variables can be used to extract and alter data from any console of any primitive.

Node Type	Name String	Variable Name
The Shape Node	"NS1Shape"	$NS1H[0]
The Make Node	"makeNurbsSphere1"	$NS1H[1]
The SG Node	"initialShadingGroup"	$NS1SG[0]
The Shader Node	"lambert1"	$NS1SH[0]

Conclusions from Attributing and Nodes

Data extraction from existing objects is the most crucial task for generating live effects. If a code can autonomously determine the location, size, geometric composition, rendering settings, and specialized characteristics in a few lines and arrays, there is little to hard-code for generating simulators. Emergent simulations require Transform Node characteristics like location, orientation, velocity, and extents calculation, while evolutionary tasks are accomplished by assessing Make and Shape Node values. Representational values are applied by unlocking Shader node characteristics and forcing numbers to visualize. This is just the tip of the iceberg.

Chapter 10

Sub-Geometry
pointPosition
NURBS Surfaces
    Non-modifiable, Modifiable Control Vertices
    Rebuilding U's and V's
    Retrieving Spans
Polygons
    Reducing and Increasing Faces
    PolyEvaluate
Subdivision Surfaces and Scripting Issues
Subdivision Lists with Wildcards

Sub-Geometry
As stated in Chapter 6, primitives are either NURBS surfaces, polygon meshes or subdivision surfaces. These surfacing types appear to be similar forms but comprehensively differ in their texturing. NURBS (grid surfaces) tend to have smooth forms, polygons (meshes) contain sharp edges and sub-d's (subdivisions) share both characteristics. Each type has advantages and disadvantages for animation and effects generation.

Attributes are one way of altering the global characteristics on primitives, like scale, radii, sweeps, and so on. These are numerical modifiers that do not change the recognizable concept of a cylinder, cone, plane, sphere, or cube, but rather they stretch, open, position and orient the shape. Modifying the elements of a primitive geometrically, as opposed to numerically, is accomplished by manipulating the "sub-geometry" of the surface. Some geometric characteristics of surfaces are vertices, edges, faces, isoparms and many more. Manipulation of sub-geometry is the process of transforming an object from one primitive-type to another.

Each surface has a collection of construction points that drive the overall shape of the form. These are influence points that are generally hidden from view when rendered, but are designed to be "control vertices" for manual manipulation. Called "cv's," they act like tiny magnets in space, that pull on parent surfaces and meshes. By transforming the configuration of cv's, any primitive can be molded from a standardized object to a dynamic and sculpted work of art.

pointPosition
With the exception of the transform commands, one command stands above all others with respect to geometry reporting. This command "pointPosition" will

always return the world space location of a point. Most sections in this chapter will require the use of this operation.

Querying the pivot and returning the translate location are good ways of getting the world space coordinate but because they can conflict, there is no guarantee the retrieved XYZ is actually correct. The command "pointPosition" is extremely stabile and disregards the history of the parent objects. Instead, it queries the desired point locator and calculates its position from the origin.

NURBS Surfaces
Just as a review, a simple grid comprises all NURBS surfaces. Users can think of a gridded sheet of paper as a great representation of NURBS surfacing. This sheet has one direction in the long axis and another direction in the short. When placed on a table, this sheet is flat and similar to a NURBS plane. When the top is taped to the bottom, a cylinder is generated. When rotated around a point on the sheet, a cone results. Even stretched forms like spheres and toruses are based on this paper logic, with a little imagination. If a person crumpled the sheet into a complex mess of crinkles, the gridded paper would still retain its long and short axes.

The axes of our fictitious sheet are defined by the letters U and V. Each U- and V-direction has a set number of divisions, expressed as lines called "isoparms." This sets the resolution of the surface, because control vertices reside at intersections of these U and V isoparms. These vertices are the means of altering this geometry. Once any surface has been created, its sub-geometry can be exposed by pressing the button "F8." This button also suppresses this view setting.

Non-modifiable, Modifiable Control Vertices
Control vertices (cv's) fall into two groups: non-modifiable and modifiable. Modifiers are driver points that influence the overall shape of the form. Non-modifiable points are locators floating on the surface and return only location and other properties. To test these NURBS points, the use of Code 10A will be required. The code will introduce three spheres of differing isoparm resolutions into the scene.

```
// Code 10A //
sphere -r 3 -n "MN1";
sphere -r 1.5 -s 20 -p 4 4 0 -n "RB1";
sphere -r 2 -nsp 18 -p -4 4 0 -n "SP1";
// Code 10A //
```

Since sub-geometry is similar to attributing, in the sense that both are components of a parent object, the syntax for unlocking sub-elements is the same. The name of the object and the sub-geometry indicator is separated with a period. The index of the U and V coordinate follows.

[Object Name] + . + [Sub-Geom Indicator] + [U][V]

For example, the object "MN1" has four U-directional and eight V-direction curves. This produces a grid of 56 CV points, because default cv locations require three more U-directional points to complete the sphere curvature. The syntax simulates a matrix array, but should not be construed as one. The indices of this pseudo-matrix are integers. If a user wished to examine the second U-cv and fifth V-cv, the name of that object is...

```
MN1.cv[1][4]
```

Users can highlight any point object by using the "select" command. Highlighted points can be moved, rotated, and scaled, but their main function is for visual confirmation. Scripters doing calculations can use this property for geometric debugging.

```
select -r MN1.cv[1][4];
```

To return the world space location of this point object, use the "pointPosition" command...

```
pointPosition MN1.cv[1][4];
// Result: -3 -0.59975 0.59975 //
```

The object "SP1" has a UV coordinate matrix of 21 and 8, respectively. "RB1" has 7 U's and 20 V's. These values were established when the sphere was created. U-coordinate counts are determined by the flag "–s" and V-coordinate by "-nsp."

```
select -r SP1.cv[20][7] ;
select -tgl RB1.cv[6][19] ;
```

By placing an integer for the U and an integer for the V, a control vertex is highlighted. Multiple cv's can be selected by using a colon. This process will produce a row or patch of cv's which can be moved, rotated or scaled. It should be noted that "pointPosition" cannot be used with row or patch strings.

To select a V-row of points...
```
select -r SP1.cv[0:5][7] ;
```
Result: *The first six cv's from row 8 on object "SP1" are highlighted.*

To select a U-row of points...
```
select -r SP1.cv[2][3:7] ;
```
Result: *The last five cv's from column 3 on object "SP1" are highlighted.*

To select a patch of points on a NURBS surface...
```
select -r SP1.cv[0:5][3:7] ;
```
Result: *A patch of points on object "SP1" are highlighted.*

Knowing the control vertex is selectable, query-able and transformable, it is considered a modifiable CV. The "sub-geometry indicator" string for a modifiable point is…

```
.cv
```

There are some limitations to this designation. Only integer indices can be utilized; no interpolation can be accomplished. Also, since these are "influential" and not directly on the surface, CV points tend to float inside or outside of the actual surface. If users want to find a point on the surface, they should use the following "sub-geometry indicator."

```
.uv
```

The drawback to the "uv" indicator is that this is read-only. Users can select this point-on-surface, but they cannot move, rotate or scale these objects.

```
select -r MN1.uv[0][3];
```
Result: *A read-only point on object "MN1" is highlighted.*

The "uv" indicator, in most cases, is used when determining the XYZ location of points on a surface. These points-on-surface are not beholden to integer indices, and floats can be utilized to interpolate between isoparms.

```
select -r MN1.uv[0.9][3.5];
```
Result: *An interpolated read-only point on object "MN1" is highlighted.*

Rebuilding U's and V's
Once a NURBS object has been created, there are two ways to alter its U and V isoparm count. Altering these values allows scripters to manipulate the resolution of a surface to handle more complexity in the middle of a process. One way to change the isoparms is to unlock the attributes of spans and sections on the object's Make Node. Each primitive has a its own sectioning flags, so use the listAttr command to confirm this utilization.

```
setAttr makeNurbSphere3.spans 25;
setAttr makeNurbSphere3.sections 25;
```
Result: *The object "SP1" has a denser isoparm layout (25x25).*

Also, U and V patterns can be altered by literally *rebuilding* them. The command "rebuildSurface" constructs an intermediate node representing the old transform object with a new U and V isoparm system. Effectly, the surface has a greater (or lesser) density of curves.

The command is relatively simple, with five flags of distinction:
-ch   Construction History
-su   U-sections
-du   U-surface degree setting

-sv   V-sections
-du   U-surface degree setting

```
rebuildSurface -ch 1 -su 15 -du 3 -sv 15 -dv 3 -dir 2 "MN1";
```
Result: *The object "MN1" has a denser isoparm layout (15x15).*

Retrieving Spans
As stated in the previous chapter, the Shape Node controls the read-only attribute of spans. They are broken down into "spansU," "spansV" and "spansUV," and return either an integer or two-element integer array.

```
getAttr RB1Shape.spansU;
// Result: 4 //
getAttr RB1Shape.spansV;
// Result: 20 //
getAttr RB1Shape.spansUV;
// Result: 4 20 //
```

These values are extremely important. For instance, if a batch action is to be written to cycle through all of the cv's of a NURBS surface, then the extents of the loop must be established. The "spans" can be stored as integers and the end condition in a loop, so multi-value isoparm counts can be analyzed in a scene.

```
int $RBsp2[1] = `getAttr RB1Shape.spansUV`;
for ($i=0;$i<($RBsp2[0]+3);$i++) {
       move -r 0 0 1 RB1.cv[$i][9];
}
```
Result: *The object "RB1" has a row of CV's that moved up 1 unit.*

Polygons
While NURBS geometry is locked into a rigid grid framework, polygons are free-form point clouds. Polygons do not have a U and V matrix, but rather just a single index input. This is stored as a list, starting with zero and ending with the polygon point count. Also, polygons retain more manipulation capabilities by exposing point, edge and face modifiers. All of these characteristics are readable and writable.

As stated in the chapter on primitives, polygons are similar to disco balls. They are faceted forms, that when observed from a distance, appear smooth. Upon closer inspection, the object is made up of several hundred pieces of flat glass. Working with polygons gives the ability to push and pull these pieces of glass without tearing. Users can take any primitive and make exciting, dynamic shapes.

The next sections on faceted geometry require the use of a sample code for file setup. This script is called "Code 10B"

```
//Code 10B//
polySphere -r 1 -sx 12 -sy 11 -n "POLY55";
move -r 3 -4 -1;
```

```
polyTorus -r 1 -sr 0.5 -tw 0 -sx 14 -sy 13 -n "POLY99";
move -r -3.25 -4.5 1;
//Code 10B//
```

The syntax for requesting a polygon point is nearly identical to NURBS cv's but with two changes: the indicator string is different and only one index is required. Polygons may or may not have a grid structure, and in most cases, they can have more than four edges coming into a point, unlike NURBS geometry.

[Object Name] + . + [Sub-Geom Indicator] + [n]

The "sub-geometry indicators" for the vertex, edge and face are as follows:

For points:	`.vtx`	`POLY55.vtx[22]`
For edges:	`.e`	`POLY99.e[33]`
For faces:	`.f`	`POLY55.f[27]`

Recognizing all of these objects are modifiable and read-able, vertices, edges and faces can be selected and manipulated like other control vertices and transform objects. When moving vertices, only one point is altered. When moving edges, two points (the end and beginning vertices) are translated simultaneously. For face movement, three or four connected points are altered together. This manipulation depends upon if the polygon is set to have triangles or quadrilaterals.

```
select -r POLY55.vtx[22];
select -tgl POLY99.e[33];
select -tgl POLY55.f[27];
move -r 0 -1 0.8;
```

Also, the pointPosition can be extracted as well.

```
float $RD_pos[] = `pointPosition POLY55.vtx[27]`;
// Result: 2.622125 -4.654861 -1.654498 //
```

Edges and faces are collections of points, so "pointPosition" will not work. Modelers who manipulate meshes by component-mode face selection often confuse the center point as a query-able point object. This is not the case.

Rows and patches of vertices can be obtained by using the colon character. This will retrieve all of the valid vertex indices between the start and end integers.

```
select -r POLY55.vtx[5:22];
```
Result: *The object "POLY55" will have its fifth, sixth, seventh...22nd vertices selected.*

Reducing and Increasing Faces

Users will inevitably need to reduce or increase the number of faces of a mesh. Some meshes are too dense to manipulate and others are too chunky to produce a realistic effect. Like NURBS geometry, the mesh resolution can be altered via the Make Node. Most polygon primitives have a similar grid to NURBS U and V isoparms, but are called "Axis," "Width," "Cap" and "Height."

```
setAttr "polySphere1.subdivisionsAxis" 18;
setAttr "polySphere1.subdivisionsHeight" 19;
setAttr "polyTorus1.subdivisionsAxis" 17;
setAttr "polyTorus1.subdivisionsHeight" 18;
```
Result: *The objects "POLY55" and "POLY99" are altered to have an increased number of vertices.*

The aforementioned attributes of density work for primitives only. If the mesh is imported into the scene from a different application or if the construction history was altered on a standard polygon shape, then altering the mesh resolution can be accomplished with the use of the commands "polyReduce" and "polySmooth." The operation "polyReduce" will remove an equal distribution of vertices across a mesh, and "polySmooth" will introduce an interpolated population of vertices into a collection of faces.

```
polyReduce -percentage 50 -t 0 -rpo 1 -ch 1 "POLY99";
```
Result: *The object "POLY99" is altered to have only ninety vertices.*

```
polySmooth -mth 1 -sl 1 -dpe 2 -ro 10 -ch 1 POLY99;
```
Result: *The object "POLY99" is smoothed to have only 910 vertices.*

PolyEvaluate

When scripting effects with polygon vertices, edges and faces, the overall sub-geometry count is paramount. Since mesh sub-geometry syntax requires only one index (unlike NURBS, which has two), looping is relatively simple. Without the vertex count, coders cannot determine the end condition of a loop.

There exists a very useful and universal command called "polyEvaluate." This command has several functions which can be found in the command reference, but this manual will just focus on the integer data from the following flags: -v, -vertex; -e, -edge; -f, -face.

```
int $VCt[] = `polyEvaluate -v POLY55`;
// Result: 326 //
int $ECt[] = `polyEvaluate -e POLY55`;
// Result: 666 //
int $FCt[] = `polyEvaluate -f POLY55`;
// Result: 342 //
```

It should be noted all polyEvaluate values will be returned in an integer array variable, even though the array is one element long. When using the variable, coders should always place zero in the index position. In the example below, the array variable "$VCt" will count the vertices on object "POLY55." Then each vertex will be move a relative distance in the Y-direction.

```
int $VCt[] = `polyEvaluate -v POLY55`;
for ($r=0;$r<$VCt[0];$r++) {
        move -r 0 ($r/100) 0 POLY55.vtx[$r];
        currentTime $r;
}
```

Result: *The object "POLY55" has several vertices moving at variable distances in the Y-direction.*

Subdivision Surfaces and Scripting Issues

The last geometry type is the subdivision surface, often abbreviated to "sub-d." This surface is basically a smoothed polygon, which is completely freeform. Unencumbered by a rigid UV grid, a single sub-d surface can take on any shape, much like clay can be sculpted into any topology.

Subdivision surfaces are generally designed for manual manipulation. As with sub-d primitive creation commands, sub-d sub-geometry commands are extremely limited. It is a best practice to avoid subdivision scripting and reserve any manipulation for manifold NURBS surfaces and/or polygonalized meshes. All surfacing types can ultimately be converted to an alternative if necessary. However, some vertex and face syntax will wrap up this chapter.

This section will use the sample code "CODE 10C" for testing.

```
// CODE 10C //
CreateSubdivSphere;
string $tempSel[] = `ls-sl`;
rename $tempSel[0] "SUBD1";
move -r 0 7 0;
CreateSubdivTorus;
string $tempSel[] = `ls-sl`;
rename $tempSel[0] "SUBD2";
move -r 3 7 0;
// CODE 10C //
```

Subdivision surfaces use a two-member matrix, which at first glance, appears to match the criteria of NURBS control vertices. Unfortunately, the simplicity of NURBS U's and V's does not translate into sub-d's. Where NURBS UV coordinates begin with zero and end with the last isoparm, sub-d coordinates have a complex numbering system. Some vertices in a sub-d may have a [0][0] value, and the very next value could be [2][256]. These numbers jump randomly and often end with indices well into the hundreds of thousands.

When examining the object "SUBD1," the following points are found:

```
SUBD1.smp[0][0]
SUBD1.smp[0][1]
SUBD1.smp[0][2]
```

```
SUBD1.smp[0][3]
SUBD1.smp[256][2]
SUBD1.smp[256][3]
SUBD1.smp[512][2]
SUBD1.smp[512][3]
```

All default sub-d spheres have eight control vertices. Users can use "pointPosition" and the transform commands to read and move the points, just like NURBS or polygon geometry. However, the matrix can often change randomly when subdivision counts are altered. Automation of this process can be extremely difficult, so it is advised to store the name-strings of all current control vertices and never alter the topology of parent sub-d object.

Subdivision Lists with Wildcards

Clearly the matrix is not linear, so the use of loops is nearly impossible when controlling vertices. There exists no command to return a list or count of sub-d vertices into an array. However, a workaround to retrieving a list of sub-d points is by querying with wildcard characters.

```
string $SubL[] = `ls SUBD1.smp["*"]`;
//Result: SUBD1.smp[0][0:3] SUBD1.smp[256][2:3]
SUBD1.smp[512][2:3] //
```

There are two drawbacks to this syntax: grouped points and no concatenation. When wildcards are used to make lists, often closely ordered numbers get named with colon characters. Instead of printing a single string per point (i.e. SUBD1.smp[0][0], SUBD1.smp[0][1], SUBD1.smp[0][2], SUBD1.smp[0][3]), the application will combine them into one string (SUBD1.smp[0][0:3]). Another disadvantage to wildcards is scripters cannot concatenate the list string with a variable name. Wildcards must be encapsulated with quotes, so this conflicts with other strings when concatenating.

Chapter 11

Animation and Keyframing
Playing the Timeline
Simulated Manual Keyframing
Scripted Keyframing
Cameras
      Clipping Planes
Background Colors
Lights

Animation and Keyframing
Previous chapters have dealt with three-dimensional modeling, but ultimately Maya is for animating. Most scenes undergo a standard sequence for the animation process: planning, modeling, animating, and rendering. The remainder of this book will reveal how this geometry can be dynamic and captured in a higher resolution sequence.

Animating is the process of taking geometric elements and setting them into motion. Scripters can animate any characteristic of an object, like its location, orientation, and size. When the movement is desired, the "translate" attribute requires numerical modification. Orientation and size can be dynamic when the "rotate" and "scale" attributes are animated.

When a characteristic needs to be animated, values are saved at specific instances in time. This process of locking characteristics in time is called "keyframing." When users play the timeline, previously keyframed attributes interpolate and drive objects in space. One can look at the flight plan of an airplane to imagine keyframing attributes. The pilot is given a series of values at specific times in the flight. These directions control the position ("translate" attribute) and the orientation ("rotate" attribute) of the plane and are provided to the pilot via the control tower at stages in the flight path.

Playing the Timeline

The fourth dimension of animating is time. Once an object has been created, it has the potential to occupy any place in the scene at any time. Users can specify, by keyframing, where the object will be and when. Before keyframing can occur, scripters must learn the process of playing, modifying, using, and adjusting the timeline.

The timeline is a bar across the bottom of the user interface. It houses dozens of hashlines and resembles a yardstick. Users can alter the spacing, beginning and end points of this timeline, which change the duration and resolution of time for the active scene. Each hashmark corresponds to a "frame" in the scene, and depending upon a user's settings, thirty frames comprise a second. The command "playbackOptions" allows coders to extend or stretch the timeline of the scene. These pertain to the "minTime" and "maxTime" which bound the visible timeline, and the "animationEndTime" and "animationStartTime" which encapsulate the scene's total timeline.

To make changes to the timeline...

```
playbackOptions -ast 0;
playbackOptions -min 1;
playbackOptions -max 777;
playbackOptions -aet 888;
```
Result: *The timeline has increased to end at the frame 777 and complete at frame 888.*

Once the bounds of the timeline are established, navigating time must be explained. The command "currentTime" acts like a panning or zooming for the fourth dimension. Previous example codes have been using "currentTime" to visualize the code, a secondary functionality of the command. Its appropriate use is to set the current value of time to a float. The number corresponds to the frame of the scene.

To move the timeslider to a specific time ...

```
currentTime 66;
```
Result: *The timeslider has been moved to frame 66.*

Variables can be used when setting the timeslider.

```
float $CT3 = 57.2;
currentTime $CT3;
```
Result: *The timeslider has been moved to frame 57.2.*

Simulated Manual Keyframing

Keyframing can be accomplished either by manual or scripted processes. The process of keyframing an attribute is as follows:

1.)   Set the start time

2.)   Change the attribute value
3.)   Set the attribute
4.)   Return to Step 1 until all values have been set.

It is imperative users follow this sequence exactly, for if time changes occurred prior to the attribute alteration, the value is nullified. Locking the keyframe is programmed with the command "setKeyframe." Modelers can use the same sequence manually by pressing the lowercase letter "s" whenever an attribute has been altered at a specific frame.

To set the translate value in time…

```
sphere -r 1.75 -n "JK1";
currentTime 66;                                        //Set time
setAttr "JK1.translate" -type "double3" 3 7 -2;        //Set attr
setKeyframe {"JK1"};                                   //Set key

currentTime 99;                                        //Set time
setAttr "JK1.translate" -type "double3" -5 0 10;       //Set attr
setKeyframe {"JK1"};                                   //Set key
```

Once this sample code has been executed and the "play" button is depressed, the scene animates. The sphere "JK1" moves diagonally across the viewport until frame 99. To reassess the code, at frame 66 the object is moved to (3, 7, -2) and set. Then the code moves the timeslider to frame 99, where a new translate value is established. Since no attributes have been keyframed after frame one-hundred, the timeline skips ahead until another attribute is found. All timelines repeat at the maximum condition, so object "JK1" will repetitively move from (3, 7, -2) to (-5, 0, 10) until the timeslider is stopped.

Individuals can keyframe an object nearly an infinite amount of times. Here is another example where the translate attribute is set four times and the rotate attribute is set twice.

```
string $CurList[] = `ls "JK*"`;
if (size($CurList)!=0) delete $CurList;
sphere -r 1.75 -n "JK1";

currentTime 66;
setAttr "JK1.translate" -type "double3" 3 7 -2;
setKeyframe {"JK1"};

currentTime 99;
setAttr "JK1.translate" -type "double3" -5 0 10;
setKeyframe {"JK1"};

currentTime 169;
setAttr "JK1.translate" -type "double3" 0 0 -4;
setAttr "JK1.rotate" -type "double3" 10 900 -50;
setKeyframe {"JK1"};
```

```
currentTime 239;
setAttr "JK1.translate" -type "double3" 4 0 -4;
setAttr "JK1.rotate" -type "double3" 1000 -420 -50;
setKeyframe {"JK1"};
```

Scripted Keyframing

As stated, the previous section details the procedure for manual keyframing. While this is the process for modelers to animate objects, it is very slow and expensive for coding purposes. Whenever a script uses the command "currentTime," the program uses memory to refresh the display and this will eat up a fraction of a second. This may appear to be negligible, but set in a loop, tens of thousands of "currentTime" executions will aggregate into hours of processing time.

The developers have provided a solution to this resource depletion by using the command "setKeyframe" more extensively. By clever flag placement, coders can set keys directly without "setAttr" or "currentTime." There are three extremely important flags:

```
-t     or     -time
-at    or     -attribute
-v     or     -value
```

The "time" is a misnomer; this is better expressed as the frame. This number will place a keyframe at the specified frame. "Attribute" and "value" are strings and floats, respectively. Coders can only place singular attribute types (as opposed to array types, like ".translate" or ".rotate") into the string and the other flag loads the value.

```
setKeyframe -t 570 -at "translateX" -v 10 JK1;
```
Result: *The object "JK1" has a single X translate keyframe of 10 units at frame 570.*

The flags "-at" and "-v" can be repeated endlessly to set several attributes simultaneously. In the next example, both the X and Y translate attributes are set.

```
setKeyframe -t 570 -at "translateX" -v 10 -at "translateY" -v -5 JK1
```
Result: *The object "JK1" has a X translate keyframe of 10 units and Y translate of -5 units at frame 570.*

Cameras

As with all animated scenes, cameras play an important role in capturing dynamic behavior. In Maya, cameras are abstract objects that behave similarly to real camcorders. Users can choose between perspective and orthogonal projections, focal lengths and other optical characteristics. All scenes have default cameras that correspond to the standard viewports and cannot be deleted, however, more cameras can be inserted into the scene.

All scenes have four default cameras: "top," "front," "side," and "persp." The first three are orthogonal views, where the field of view is parallel. Objects in an orthogonal viewport may appear as if the viewer is looking at them through a telescope. Perspective cameras have settings which simulate vanishing points. These comprise the four main viewports in the user interface.

Selecting a camera is extremely important, because it will open up tabs on the user interface. Since the camera is the viewport, there is nothing to select with a mouse. Users must either script the selection...

```
select -r persp;
```

or to manually select a camera in its own viewport, use the following viewport menu sequence...

View > Select Camera...

Cameras can be moved in two ways. Users can use the mouse navigation techniques described in the first chapter, like panning, zooming and orbiting, or the camera object itself can be moved or rotated into place. Cameras, like geometry, have transform nodes, so the default xform matrix applies. To move a camera using the transform commands...

```
move -r 4 4 1 persp;
rotate -r 10 10 -10 persp;
```
Result: *The camera "persp" has been moved (4, 4, 1) units from its current location and rotated.*

Attributes can also be set to move or orient the camera.

```
setAttr persp.translate -type "double3" 5 -5 5;
```
Result: *The camera "persp" has been moved to the location (5, -5, 5).*

Additionally cameras have Shape Nodes which house a list of important visual attributes unique to its object type. Like real cameras, any perspective has a variable focal length; this value determines how far the lens will bend or "fish-eye" the scene.

```
setAttr "perspShape.focalLength" 30;
```
Result: *The camera "persp" has been a normal perspective.*

```
setAttr "perspShape.focalLength" 13;
```
Result: *The camera "persp" has been a fish-eye perspective.*

Clipping Planes
The clipping plane determines the visual depth of the scene. For example, when a person places a note card too close to their face, the words are not readable. Conversely, if the note card is a mile away, it is too far to be intelligible. This is the premise of the clipping plane and the application hides all objects beyond its visual extents.***

Scripters can witness the issues with clipping planes in this example…

```
for ($i=0;$i<200;$i++) {
        sphere -p ($i*160) 0 0 -r 12 -n ("SP"+$i);
}
```
Result: *200 spheres have been created along the X axis, but only a few appear in the scene.*

In the previous code, two hundred spheres were generated. To prove this, a coder could use the "ls -tr" command to print the list of 200 objects. However, upon visual inspection of the viewport, only a dozen appear in the scene. The far clipping plane has a default setting of 1000 units, so nearly all objects are being hidden by the application to save resources. Users can increase the viewable area by…

```
setAttr "perspShape.nearClipPlane" 1;
setAttr "perspShape.farClipPlane" 1000000;
```
Result: *All 200 spheres appear in the scene.*

Background Colors
Each camera has its own background color. This is an attribute of type color residing in the Shape Node of a perspective or orthogonal camera. These colors may not appear in the viewport window, but will be exceedingly important in the process of exporting the scene in high resolution images. The attribute

---

*** Beginners are tempted to increase the far clipping plane to an extremely large value, to ensure that any objects created or imported into the scene will always be visible. If a very large value is required (over 1000000 units), it is advised that users also increase the near clipping plane value. The near plane value should not be less than six significant digits of the far plane, otherwise artifacts in the rendering process will result.

behind this functionality is called "backgroundColor," and it requires an RGB array as inputs.

```
setAttr "perspShape.backgroundColor" -type double3 0.9 0 0 ;
```
Result: *The background of the camera is set to a red tone.*

Lights

As with real photography, lighting is paramount. Without any light, every rendering and animation would be completely dark, even if the scene had thousands of objects. Scripters can place lights anywhere in a scene and adjust their intensity for optimal effects.

To view the light exposure in a file, the viewport settings must be altered. Most files default to either a wireframe or shaded view, but two other shaded settings exist. These can be established manually or through scripting. When using the command "DisplayLight," the model will shift from a shaded view to a light exposure view.[†††]

Scripted	User Interface
`DisplayWireframe;`	`//Press "4"`
`DisplayShaded;`	`//Press "5"`
`DisplayShadedAndTextured;`	`//Press "6"`
`DisplayLight;`	`//Press "7"`

There exists a catalog of light sources, each with differing ways of radiating illumination. A directional light provides illumination with each ray parallel, much like light from the sun strikes the earth. Point light sources are similar to incandescent bulbs, where the beams radiate concentrically until hitting a surface. Spot lights simulate theatre lamps, because they have a start point and direction. Lastly, area lights spread illumination across a representational rectangle, much like drop-ceiling office light covers diffuse the light from fluorescent bulbs. All light types are created by the same command, called "shadingNode." The flag "-asLight" designates the light source with the following strings:

```
shadingNode -asLight directionalLight;
shadingNode -asLight pointLight;
shadingNode -asLight spotLight;
shadingNode -asLight areaLight;
```

Directional lights require only the orientation, because all rays are parallel, the location of the source is irrelevant. Coders can scale this source, but it is merely a representational icon.

```
DisplayShaded;
DisplayLight;
```

[†††] When working with a wireframe model, "DisplayLight" must be executed after a shading command.

```
sphere -r 4 -p 9 1 -1 -n "YU1";
shadingNode -asLight directionalLight -n "DIRLIGHT1";
rotate -r -os 20 0 0 "DIRLIGHT1";
scale -r 100 100 100 "DIRLIGHT1";
```
Result: *A directional light named "DIRLIGHT1" is created and oriented 20 degrees off the X axis.*

Point lights are very easy to install and are probably the most popular illumination objects. They radiate in all directions, much like standard household lamps.

```
DisplayShaded;
DisplayLight;
sphere -r 4 -p 9 1 -1 -n "YU1";
shadingNode -asLight pointLight -n "PTLIGHT1";
move -r 4 4 4 "PTLIGHT1";
```
Result: *A point light named "PTLIGHT1" is created and moved to (4, 4, 4).*

When the scene calls for a certain object to be illuminated, a spot light is the best localized light source. The location and orientation of these lamps are paramount, because objects outside of the extents of the light's focus will remain in shadows. Also, with a simple change of the "coneAngle" attribute, users can narrow or expand the width of the spot light.

```
DisplayShaded;
DisplayLight;
sphere -r 4 -p 9 1 -1 -n "YU1";
shadingNode -asLight spotLight -n "SPOTLIGHT1";
move -r 7 4 10 "SPOTLIGHT1";
rotate -r -20 -20 10 "SPOTLIGHT1";
scale -r 100 100 100 "SPOTLIGHT1";
setAttr "SPOTLIGHT1.coneAngle" 25;
```
Result: *A spot light named "SPOTLIGHT1" is created and moved to (7, 4, 10) and rotated slightly. Also, its "coneAngle" was narrowed to 25 degrees.*

Area lights are rectangles that emit light. Since this is similar to a nurbsPlane, the translate, rotate and scale attributes are main drivers.

```
DisplayShaded;
DisplayLight;
sphere -r 4 -p 9 1 -1 -n "YU1";
shadingNode -asLight areaLight -n "AREALIGHT1";
move -r 7 4 10 "AREALIGHT1";
scale -r 100 10 1 "AREALIGHT1";
```
Result: *A spot light named "AREALIGHT1" is created and moved to (7, 4, 10).*

All lights have different attributes complimenting its respective type. However all share the characteristics of "intensity" and "decayRate." The intensity requires a float to determine how bright the light is, much like the wattage of denotes the luminosity in incandescent bulbs. When default lights are greater than a value of one, extreme contrast may result in renderings. Use large intensity values with care.

```
setAttr "AREALIGHT1.intensity" 1.405;
```
Result: *The existing light "AREALIGHT1" has increased its brightness from 1 to 1.405.*

The decay rate pertains to the way light radiates from a source. There are four settings designated with integers: 0, "No Decay;" 1, "Linear;" 2, "Quadratic;" and 3, "Cubic." Without any decay (which is the default for all lights), light rays will emit endlessly throughout the scene, artificially illuminating objects equally, even if they are nearby or thousands of units away. To avoid this artificial aesthetic, coders can set the decay to the latter three values. Real electromagnetic emitters broadcast their signal with a quadratic decay, where the energy is spread in a inverse square function.

```
setAttr PTLIGHT1.decayRate 0;
setAttr PTLIGHT1.decayRate 1;
setAttr PTLIGHT1.decayRate 2;
setAttr PTLIGHT1.decayRate 3;
```

Chapter 12

Materials and Rendering
Shaders
Connecting Shaders to Geometry
Standard Shader Attributes
Querying Shaders from Materials
Image Project Set Directory
The Rendering Process
Default Render Globals
Raytracing: Reflectance and Shadows
Rendering Commands
Dedicated Render Counters
Default Render Globals and Animation
Batch Rendering (Keyframed Rendering)

Materials and Rendering
The last stage of producing an animation is capturing the scene in a high resolution format. The viewport resolution is a draft, working environment which is very abstract or abbreviated. Designers need to convert this draft visualization into a clear, production quality representation. This can be finalized in the form of an image, series of images, or a video. This conversion process is called rendering.

High-quality images, called renderings, finalize the animation process. When a snapshot of the scene is captured, this is a singular rendering. When thousands of renderings are placed in a sequence and are played as a video, this is called an animation.

The scene goes through many preparatory measures between the initial creation of geometry and final process of rendering. As stated in the previous chapter, cameras and lights must be placed and set into the file. Also, each object will be given a material called a shader. Lastly, a series of image properties will be set to specify the quality of the image or video. All of these factors (geometry, cameras, lights, shaders, and image settings) work in concert to make a production quality rendering.

Shaders
Shaders are materials applied to surfaces. These can be as simple as solid colors or as complex as tiled patterns. Basic materials are categorized by their "specularity," a characteristic best described as the spectrum of shiny to mat finish. The materials "Blinn" and "Phong" are quite shiny, while the "Lambert" is a flat mat finish. All objects by default enter a scene with a mat finish, called

"lambert1." Users must replace this default material with either a Blinn, Phong or another Lambert to change the initial color.

Many objects can share the same shader. If a scene had seven cubes which needed to be yellow, only one material would need to be created with the designated color. Then this singular shader would color all cubes in the file. However, if the scripter desired a rainbow color scheme, with each cube having a separate tone, a different shader would need to be created for the spectrum.

Using the command "shadingNode," coders can create either a blinn, lambert or phong material type. The flag "-asShader" requires the name string to make this determination.

```
shadingNode -asShader blinn -n BMat7;
shadingNode -asShader lambert -n LambertNP37;
shadingNode -asShader phong -n PHONG_Test276;
```
Result: *A blinn material named "BMat7," lambert material named "LambertNP37," and phong material named "PHONG_Test276."*

Connecting Shaders to Geometry
Once geometry comes into the picture, shader creation is more complex than simple transformation or primitive commands. Just merely creating the shader does not establish a functioning material for geometry; it must be connected with the commands "sets" and "connectAttr" to make the object renderable. Shaders work based on connections, so a sequence of lines must follow all "shadingNode" commands. The creation of an object called a Shader Group acts as the intermediary between the material and the geometry. Without this connection, the material will not appear on the surface. The follow four-step process shows a typical material transition:

Preliminary Geometry:
```
DisplayShaded;
sphere -r 10 -p 2 2 2 -n "CObj7";
```
Result: *A sphere called "CObj7" was created, but it has the grey default "lambert1" applied.*

Step 1.)
```
shadingNode -asShader blinn -n blinn1;
```
Result: *The blinn material called "blinn1" was created.*

Step 2.)
```
sets -renderable true -noSurfaceShader true -empty -name blinn1SG;
```
Result: *The shader group "blinn1SG" was created.*

Step 3.)
```
connectAttr -f blinn1.outColor blinn1SG.surfaceShader;
```
Result: *The shader and shader group are connected.*

Step 4.)

```
sets -e -forceElement blinn1SG CObj7;
```
Result: *The "blinn1" is applied to the object "CObj7" via the Shader Group "blinn1SG."*

To summarize, here is the condensed code from above:
```
DisplayShaded;
sphere -r 10 -p 2 2 2 -n "CObj7";
shadingNode -asShader blinn -n blinn1;
sets -renderable true -noSurfaceShader true -empty -name blinn1SG;
connectAttr -f blinn1.outColor blinn1SG.surfaceShader;
sets -e -forceElement blinn1SG CObj7;
```

The previous sequence shows how a hard-coded material named "blinn1" could be connected to some geometry. This sequence is not very portable[‡‡‡]. The best practice for shader creation is to establish unique names for the shader and shader group. This will universalize the process, so that adding new materials is easier to modify. Also, this will allow coders to concatenate suffix numbers to names, which exposes the naming convention to loop integers.

```
// Code 12A:  Recommended Lambert Shader Application Procedure //
DisplayShaded;
sphere -r 10 -p 2 2 2 -n "CObj7";
// Adding Material
int $XCounter = 1;
string $CurPrefix = "NPLambert";
string $CurLambert = $CurPrefix + $XCounter;
string $CurLambertSG = $CurPrefix + $XCounter + "SG";
string $CurLambertSGsS = $CurPrefix + $XCounter + "SG.surfaceShader";
string $CurLambertoutColor = $CurPrefix + $XCounter + ".outColor";
shadingNode -asShader lambert -n $CurLambert;
sets -renderable true -noSurfaceShader true -empty -name $CurLambertSG;
connectAttr -f $CurLambertoutColor $CurLambertSGsS;
sets -e -forceElement $CurLambertSG CObj7;
// Code 12A //
```
Result: *A lambert material called "NPLambert1" was created and applied to object "CObj7."*

This may appear to be a lot of code just to put a material on an object, but all of the connections are necessary. Prefacing each shader with these string declarations and assignments will make coding easier in the future. Code 12A is an example of a portable lambert creation script. Code 12B and 12C display how to insert a phong and blinn material onto a geometric element, respectively.

```
// Code 12B:  Recommended Phong Shader Application Procedure //
DisplayShaded;
sphere -r 10 -p -2 2 2 -n "CObj7";
// Adding Material
int $XCounter = 1;
string $CurPrefix = "SamplePhong";
string $CurMat = $CurPrefix + $XCounter;
string $CurMatSG = $CurPrefix + $XCounter + "SG";
```

[‡‡‡] The term 'portable' pertains to how a code can accommodate more than one scenario. This is accomplished by using universalized variables and/or placing in a global procedure.

```
string $CurMatSGsS = $CurPrefix + $XCounter + "SG.surfaceShader";
string $CurMatoutColor = $CurPrefix + $XCounter + ".outColor";
shadingNode -asShader phong -n $CurMat;
sets -renderable true -noSurfaceShader true -empty -name $CurMatSG;
connectAttr -f $CurMatoutColor $CurMatSGsS;
sets -e -forceElement $CurMatSG CObj7;
// Code 12B //
```

Result: *A phong material called "SamplePhong1" was created and applied to object "CObj7."*

```
// Code 12C:  Recommended Blinn Shader Application Procedure //
DisplayShaded;
sphere -r 10 -p -2 2 2 -n "CObj7";
// Adding Material
int $XCounter = 1;
string $CurPrefix = "HB3B";
string $CurMat = $CurPrefix + $XCounter;
string $CurMatSG = $CurPrefix + $XCounter + "SG";
string $CurMatSGsS = $CurPrefix + $XCounter + "SG.surfaceShader";
string $CurMatoutColor = $CurPrefix + $XCounter + ".outColor";
shadingNode -asShader blinn -n $CurMat;
sets -renderable true -noSurfaceShader true -empty -name $CurMatSG;
connectAttr -f $CurMatoutColor $CurMatSGsS;
sets -e -forceElement $CurMatSG CObj7;
// Code 12C //
```

Result: *A phong material called "HB3B1" was created and applied to object "CObj7."*

Standard Shader Attributes

As with lights, cameras, geometry and nearly everything else in the application, shader objects have attributes. Since shaders are zero-dimensional objects, meaning they do not occupy space, they do not have a Transform, Shape or Make Node. The shader itself is the node containing all of the pertinent characteristics which comprise a material, like color, transparency, specularity, translucency, ambience, and incandescence. Also, imported images can be applied through the shader, producing patterns, textures, noise, gradients, and movies.

A user cannot place a shader at the origin or at coordinate (x, y, z); they exist in a library called the "HyperShade" and can be opened by the following methods:

To open the HyperShade Window in the user interface…
Window > Rendering Editors > HyperShade

To open the HyperShade Window via scripting…
```
HypershadeWindow;
```

Once a material has been applied to an object, coders can alter the characteristics of the shader. In general, most shader attributes are quantified as a series of floats called an "RGB" value. This stands for a combination of float numbers from zero to one, each with a designation for the red, green and blue values.

White color: RGB = (1, 1, 1)
Black color: RGB = (0, 0, 0)
Red color: RGB = (1, 0, 0)
Green color: RGB = (0, 1, 0)
Blue color: RGB = (0, 0, 1)
Yellow color: RGB = (1, 1, 0)
Magenta color: RGB = (1, 0, 1)
Cyan color: RGB = (0, 1, 1)
Grey color: RGB = (0.5, 0.5, 0.5)
Orange color: RGB = (1, 0.5, 0)
Purple color: RGB = (0.5, 0, 1)

The upcoming shader attribute examples require running Code 12C prior. That code produces a sphere and a blinn shader called "HB3B1." The default shader attributes are "color," "transparency," "ambientColor," "incandescence," "specularColor," and "glowIntensity." The ambient color deals with the intensity of the shadows, and an increased ambience will have softer dark places. Incandescence is the attribute for emitting light. High light emission values will lead to bleaching out of the material. The specular color adjusts the intensity of the reflectance and glossiness. A simulated attribute called "glowIntensity" will add a small halo around the surface depending upon the color and settings.

```
getAttr "HB3B1.color" ;
// Result: 0.5 0.5 0.5 //
getAttr "HB3B1.transparency" ;
// Result: 0 0 0 //
getAttr "HB3B1.ambientColor" ;
// Result: 0 0 0 //
getAttr "HB3B1.incandescence" ;
// Result: 0 0 0 //
getAttr "HB3B1.specularColor" ;
// Result: 0.5 0.5 0.5 //
getAttr "HB3B1.glowIntensity" ;
// Result: 0 //
```

One could question how a transparency could have a color value. Transparencies should be a gradient value from zero to one, but for consistency, the application uses the RGB format. A gradient grey value will suffice for set percentage transparency.

(0, 0, 0) transparency   = 0% clear (Opaque)
(0.25, 0.25, 0.25) transparency   = 25% clear
(0.5, 0.5, 0.5) transparency   = 50% clear
(0.75, 0.75, 0.75) transparency   = 75% clear
(1, 1, 1) transparency   = fully clear (Transparent)

Just as attributes can be retrieved from a shader, these characteristics can be modified by using the "setAttr" command. The following settings should convert the sphere object's colors to produce a material similar to the surface features of an incandescent light bulb.

To make a simulated light bulb material...
```
setAttr "HB3B1.color" -type double3 1 0.89 0.46 ;
setAttr "HB3B1.transparency" -type double3 0.12 0.12 0.12 ;
setAttr "HB3B1.ambientColor" -type double3 0.26 0.26 0.26 ;
setAttr "HB3B1.incandescence" -type double3 0.80 0.80 0.67 ;
setAttr "HB3B1.specularColor" -type double3 0.9 0.9 0.9 ;
setAttr "HB3B1.glowIntensity" 0.11;
```

Querying Shaders from Materials

All objects are made up of nodes. In previous chapters, this manual has described the procedure for navigating these nodes, starting with the Transform and ending with the Shape and Make nodes. All geometry has another node not covered until this section: the Shader node. As stated in the previous section, shaders are objects on their own, but when connected to geometry, it also becomes a part of the node list.

When created, all objects enter the scene with the default lambert material. Users can replace this lambert with any other material type, expanding the visual capabilities of the scene. Both of these statements show an object can only have two states of material mapping: initial or replaced. When querying the material from an object, both conditions require a slightly different setup.

Code 12D must be run prior to the examination of querying materials from geometry. It creates two cones, one with the default shader and another with a new blinn.

```
// Code 12D:  Setup Cones for Testing //
DisplayShaded;
cone -r 10 -p -1 -1 2 -n "DCone1";
cone -r 8 -p -10 10 4 -n "DCone2";
int $XCounter = 1;
string $CurPrefix = "CMatA";
string $CurMat = $CurPrefix + $XCounter;
string $CurMatSG = $CurPrefix + $XCounter + "SG";
string $CurMatSGsS = $CurPrefix + $XCounter + "SG.surfaceShader";
string $CurMatoutColor = $CurPrefix + $XCounter + ".outColor";
shadingNode -asShader blinn -n $CurMat;
sets -renderable true -noSurfaceShader true -empty -name $CurMatSG;
connectAttr -f $CurMatoutColor $CurMatSGsS;
sets -e -forceElement $CurMatSG DCone2;
// Code 12D //
```
Result: *Two cones called "DCone1" and "DCone2" are created. "DCone2" has a blinn material named "CMatA1" applied.*

The object named "DCone1" is a simple cone with a default shader named "lamber1" applied. This is a standard configuration for any object with no modification. Traversing the node structure for object "DCone1" is simple using the commands "listHistory" and "listConnections." By extracting the first index of all returned arrays, the name "lambert1" will be saved as a string. In the script named "Code 12E" below, the process of extraction is revealed in four lines. The final output is just printed, but in most scenarios, this value would be loaded into a string variable and saved for future calculations.

```
// Code 12E:  Retrieving Initial Material //
string $DS1H[] = `listHistory DCone1`;
string $DS1G[] = `listConnections $DS1H[0]`;
string $DS1SH[] = `listConnections $DS1G[0]`;
print $DS1SH[0];
// Code 12E //
```
Result: *The string "lamber1" is printed.*

The "Code 12E" displays the process for retrieving a shader connected to geometry with an initial material. This process works only in these cases, and replaced materials always require a slightly altered extraction process. The only change is the final connection list has a larger sequence, so the array index must correspond to this alteration. "Code 12F" below reveals the procedure for extracting a replaced material from the name of a geometrical object.

```
// Code 12F:  Retrieving Replaced Material //
string $DS1H[] = `listHistory DCone2`;
string $DS1G[] = `listConnections $DS1H[0]`;
string $DS1SH[] = `listConnections $DS1G[0]`;
print $DS1SH[3];
// Code 12F //
```
Result: *The string "CMatA1" is printed.*

Image Project Set Directory
Because the rendering process deals with the exporting of images and videos from a draft viewport, the destination of these files must be established. The application has provided a window for setting this directory, which will be the repository for all future image file formats. If left unset, all images are saved to the user folder:

...\user\My Documents\maya\projects\default\images

To manually reset the project rendering location...
File > Project > Set

To script the project rendering location...
```
sp_setLocalWorkspaceCallback "C:/DS/User/My Docs/My Pics" "directory";
```

If scripting the location of the image repository, it is imperative coders verify the destination directory exists. If not, errors will result. The potential benefit of scripting this location is coders could separate simultaneous rendering sequences into their respective directories. File management will reduce post-processing time when compiling the image sequences.

The Rendering Process

The word "rendering" can be a noun or a verb. Previous sections have expressed the term as a noun, stating that *a rendering is an image*. However, this word can also describe the act of rendering, or in other words, converting a simple outline to a finished product. For example, an artist can produce a painting by first sketching out the basic forms and then rendering the scene with a brush. To take this further, assume the artist rendered an oil painting, but four others with colored pencils, oil pastels, charcoal, and watercolors. Each painting style will impact the rendering process differently, resulting in five images of the same thing but with slightly altered atmospheres. When rendering in Maya, the application has provided a diverse array of styles of capturing the scene.

Maya has three standard rendering engines, each with completely different output styles. The first, called "Maya Software," is the default rendering type. It requires the use of lights, materials and geometry to make a typical bitmap. The second, called "Maya Vector," produces flat line drawings of the current view of the camera. The last rendering style, named "Mental Ray," simulates realistic illumination by working with virtual photons.

This chapter will only explain Maya Software for a variety of reasons. Maya Software is very clear and simple to use. The two other rendering engines require a good deal of formatting and preparation, in both the scripted and non-scripted processes. Maya Software produces ready-to-use images that can be viewed or accessed in all editing programs. Vectors require more advanced technology, about which some novice MEL scripters may not be so savvy. Maya Software renders in a short period of time, especially when the scene population is small. The duration of a Mental Ray animation can be ten to one hundred times the time spent on the same scene in Maya Software rendering.

Default Render Globals

One object controls all of the rendering characteristics of a scene for the Maya Software rendering engine. This object does not have a Transform, Make or Shape node, much like a shader and is completely abstract. Instead, it sets up the image file type extension, beginning and end frames, number of significant digits, default lighting and other image related characteristics. Named the "defaultRenderGlobals," this object has dozens of unique attributes found nowhere in the geometrical lists.

The "defaultRenderGlobals" can be expressed as a virtual photo studio. This object contains all of the important features regarding the capturing and saving of images in the scene. Some attributes include file extension padding and determination, memory management, image naming, animation duration, and presentation quality. More can be printed using the "listAttr" command:

```
listAttr defaultRenderGlobals;
// Result: message caching isHistoricallyInteresting nodeState macCodec
macDepth macQual comFrrt renderAll ignoreFilmGate quality resolution
clipFinalShadedColor enableDepthMaps enableDefaultLight enableStrokeRender
onlyRenderStrokes strokesDepthFile imageFormat pluginFormat gammaCorrection
```

```
topRegion leftRegion bottomRegion rightRegion useRenderRegion animation
animationRange startFrame endFrame byFrame byFrameStep modifyExtension
startExtension byExtension extensionPadding fieldExtControl stereoExtControl
outFormatControl oddFieldExt evenFieldExt leftStereoExt rightStereoExt
outFormatExt useMayaFileName useFrameExt putFrameBeforeExt periodInExt
imageFilePrefix composite compositeThreshold shadowsObeyLightLinking
recursionDepth leafPrimitives subdivisionPower subdivisionHashSize
logRenderPerformance geometryVector shadingVector maximumMemory numCpusToUse
interruptFrequency shadowPass iprShadowPass useFileCache optimizeInstances
reuseTessellations motionBlur motionBlurByFrame fogGeometry applyFogInPost
postFogBlur preRenderMel postRenderMel preFurRenderMel postFurRenderMel
createIprFile blurLength blurSharpness smoothValue useBlur2DMemoryCap
blur2DMemoryCap motionBlurType useDisplacementBoundingBox smoothColor
keepMotionVector iprRenderShading iprRenderShadowMaps iprRenderMotionBlur
rendercallback renderLayerEnable renderLayerPassEnable renderGlobalPassEnable
renderLayerSubdirs forceTileSize tileWidth tileHeight jitterFinalColor
raysSeeBackground oversamplePaintEffects oversamplePfxPostFilter
currentRenderer //
```

The most important attributes in the "defaultRenderGlobals" object are "imageFilePrefix," "imageFormat," "animation," "outFormatControl," "startFrame," "endFrame," "byFrameStep," "extensionPadding," "mask" and "enableDefaultLight." These consist of the basic and necessary functions of file management. All other characteristics deal with aesthetic consideration, but the basic attributes tell the application how to save the files. Without them, images could export with extensions, names, or time, rendering them useless.

Before revealing the scripted way to alter the "defaultRenderGlobals," it should be stated all of these attributes can be accessed via the "Render Globals" window in the user interface.

Window > Rendering Editors > Render Globals...

When rendering, the name of the image is paramount. This will be a string which should describe the scene.

```
setAttr defaultRenderGlobals.imageFilePrefix -type "string" "ImN007";
```
Result: *The image name will start with "ImN007".*

Next the suffix of the file must be determined. As with all files, the extension determines the file type, and thus, it determines the quality of the image. Images with a lower quality are rewarded with a smaller file size, and as the image becomes a higher resolution, the quality requires more data and larger files. Going from lowest resolution to highest, the following file extensions are industry standards: jpg, gif, bmp, tga, tif. "Maya Software" rendering can export up to twenty image types, but this manual will only cover the main file types mentioned before. The attribute reads integers, and each number stands for a different file extension string.

```
//  0:gif, 3:tif, 8:jpg, 19:tga, 20:bmp,
setAttr defaultRenderGlobals.imageFormat 8;
```
Result: *The image file will be a jpg (the low quality, but small file size, image type).*

Users can export files without any file extension by modifying the attribute "outFormatControl." This is not advised and should always be set to zero, which establishes the standard "Name.Ext" format. If set to one or two, files will be exported into in string configurations most video or image previewing programs will not recognize. To verify if the attribute is correctly set, set the "outFormatControl" to zero.

```
setAttr defaultRenderGlobals.outFormatControl 0;   //0:Regular Ext.
```
Result: *The image file will be named with the format XXXXX . xxx*

When using the TIF or TGA file extension, this format allows for the capability of generating an alpha channel mask. This is an invisible layer of image data in a file that removes the background of a scene. After the rendering has completed and saved the TIF or TGA file, a designer could open this file in an image modification program and activated the alpha channel, removing the background around the geometry. If an alpha channel is left on for the BMP, JPG or GIF formats, no errors will result.

```
setAttr "perspShape.mask" 1;
```
Result: *The alpha channel mask is turned on.*

All scenes need lights to render a scene. If no illumination sources were placed in the file, a default directional light will automatically turn on. This light generally looks fake and should not be used as the main means of luminescence. By default, this light will always be on, so users should reset the Boolean attribute to zero (false).

```
setAttr "defaultRenderGlobals.enableDefaultLight" 0;
```
Result: *The default directional light is turned off.*

Raytracing: Reflectance and Shadows
By default, all scenes begin with no reflectivity. Reflectance is the effect of light bouncing off of objects. Mirrors and chrome finish have the highest rate of reflectance, while mat finish objects reflect nothing. Also, default objects are devoid of sharp shadows, resulting in an unrealistic shading output. To turn on reflectance and crisp shadows, users must activate the rendering engine's "raytracing" capabilities. In the realm of three-dimensional modeling, this effect is extremely expensive computationally and should be used in moderation. This axiom is even more prudent for algorithmic scenarios.

To turn on reflectivity in a scene, the following lines provide an adequate setup condition...
```
setAttr "defaultRenderQuality.enableRaytracing" 1;
setAttr "defaultRenderQuality.refractions" 1;
setAttr "defaultRenderQuality.shadows" 2;
setAttr "defaultRenderQuality.reflections" 1;
```

Result: *The raytracing capabilities of the scene are turned on and set to modest values.*

Coders can turn off reflectivity by resetting the parent Boolean attribute "enableRaytracing." This will nullify all of the related aforementioned settings, and speed up rendering time.

```
setAttr "defaultRenderQuality.enableRaytracing" 0;
```
Result: *The raytracing capabilities of the scene are turned off.*

Rendering Commands
The application has two ways of capturing a scene: single image rendering and batch rendering. When users want a single image, they can request a snapshot. This process can be placed in a loop to make a series of images or animation. Also, the developers have allocated the process of rendering a sequence of images with a batch process command. All three methods are viable ways of producing high-quality images.

To make a single rendering of the current place in the timeline, use the "render" command. This command has two flags pertaining to the size of the image: "-x" and "-y." The "x" direction establishes the width of the image, and the "y" corresponds to the height. This value is an integer that stands for the number of pixels in their respective direction. Lastly, the name of the camera follows the command to determine the captured viewpoint.

```
render -x 720 -y 480 persp;
```
Result: *An 720x480 pixel image was taken by the camera "persp" at the current time.*

By placing this command line inside of a loop, users can make a sequence of renderings. This command is very useful, because any camera name can be placed in the sequence. Users can render all viewpoints in a few lines of code. This single render command is called an "in-progress" or "build-up" code[§§§], because it takes a snapshot of the current status of the model. The render line will wait for the image to complete before moving onto the next line.

```
for($x=0;$x<500;$x++) {
 currentTime $x;
 setAttr defaultRenderGlobals.imageFilePrefix -type "string" ("Im"+$x);
 render -x 720 -y 480 persp;
 setAttr defaultRenderGlobals.imageFilePrefix -type "string" ("It"+$x);
 render -x 1440 -y 960 top;
}
```
Result: *Two image sequences from frame 0 to 500 are rendered, from the "persp" and "top" view cameras.*

[§§§] A best practice for using "build-up" rendering is to comment out the render lines. Because MEL does not allow for halting the code, leaving in a render command on a test run or accidental execution will require several hours of time. Only after all setup and testing is completed, should the comments be removed.

Dedicated Render Counters

When several loops are used, "build-up" rendering requires a dedicated counter for naming. If the same counter is used again, the file does not prompt an error and saves over the file. This occurs in both sequential and nested loop configuration.

```
// Incorrect Syntax.  Do not use. //
for($x=0;$x<50;$x++) {
 for($y=0;$y<25;$y++) {
   sphere -r 0.25 -p $x $y 1 -n ("SPH"+$x+"_"+$y);
   setAttr defaultRenderGlobals.imageFilePrefix -type "string" ("Im"+$y);
   render -x 720 -y 480 persp;
 }
}
// Incorrect Syntax.  Do not use. //
```

The previous sample code will overwrite the same images every twenty-five rounds. Instead of getting 1250 (25 x 50) total images, the user will only get 25 total. Instead, coders should reserve an integer for just counting the images as they are created. This variable must always be placed after any instance the render and naming command execution. Also, as with all loops, it is helpful to print the progress of the code. Here is the correct way of rendering the previous scene.

```
int $R = 0;
for($x=0;$x<50;$x++) {
 for($y=0;$y<25;$y++) {
   print ("Rendering Completed...   " + $R + "\n");
   sphere -r 0.25 -p $x $y 1 -n ("SPH"+$x+"_"+$y);
   setAttr defaultRenderGlobals.imageFilePrefix -type "string" ("Im"+$R);
   $R++;
   render -x 720 -y 480 persp;
 }
}
```

Result: *An image sequence from 0 to 1250 is created.*

Default Render Globals and Animation

The previous sections showed how to render a singular image. The next five attributes will explain how to render an animation (a sequence of images). While a scripter could render an image sequence in a loop, generating a "build-up" animation, the application has also provided a means of batch rendering preset animations. Both are valid ways of rendering, but batch processes are generally associated with "keyframed" animations.

To toggle between rendering a single image and animation, use the "animation" attribute name.

```
setAttr defaultRenderGlobals.animation 0; //Single Rendering
setAttr defaultRenderGlobals.animation 1; //Animation Rendering
```

As with all animation rendering, the boundaries of time are important. The beginning time, end time and interval are simple float numbers which correspond directly with the timeslider activity. The "startFrame" establishes the beginning condition of the timeline and initializes the scene's keyframed elements. To determine the interval of time, the attribute "byFrameStep" is a float number; fractional inputs increase the number of frames per segment, while inputs greater than one will reduce the image count. Lastly, the attribute "endFrame" acts as the upper bound of the captured part of the timeslider.

```
setAttr "defaultRenderGlobals.startFrame" 1;
setAttr "defaultRenderGlobals.endFrame" 22;
setAttr "defaultRenderGlobals.byFrameStep" 0.5;
```
Result: *The animation settings are will render from frame 1 to frame 22, resulting in 42 total images (because the interval is 0.5).*

```
setAttr "defaultRenderGlobals.startFrame" 0;
setAttr "defaultRenderGlobals.endFrame" 400;
setAttr "defaultRenderGlobals.byFrameStep" 4;
```
Result: *The animation settings are will render from frame 0 to frame 400, resulting in 100 total images (because the interval is 4).*

Animation renderings require additional information in the file name to designate the sequence order. Since the "outFormatControl" is set to zero, file name syntax is XXXXX.xxx and XXXXX.##.xxx for singular and animation rendering sequences respectively. When users set the "startFrame," "endFrame" and "byFrameStep," the progress along the timeslider is placed in the root name of the file. i.e., the fifth frame rendering would be spelled "XXXXX.5.jpg" and the 37th frame would be "XXXXX.37.jpg." Frame 190 would be "XXXXX.190.jpg" and frame 3501 would be "XXXXX.3501.jpg." This introduces a problem when compiling these files in animation software outside of Maya: file names are sorted alphabetically, not numerically. Image 111 would come before image 3. The developers have allocated an attribute named "extensionPadding" which formats the number of the frame in the context of significant digits. If the frame padding were to be set to four digits, frame 111 would look like "XXXXX.0111.jpg" and frame 3 would be expressed as "XXXXX.0003.jpg."

```
setAttr "defaultRenderGlobals.extensionPadding" 3;
```
Result: *All resultant rendering will always have at least three digits.*

Batch Rendering (Keyframed Rendering)
The dimensions of an animated or "keyframed" image sequence are not set by the command, like in the case of "render." Instead, the "height" and "width" are set with attributes and must be preset prior to batch rendering.

```
setAttr defaultResolution.width 480;
setAttr defaultResolution.height 600;
```
Once the startFrame, endFrame, interval, width and height are set, the command "batchRender" will automatically loop through the aforementioned conditions.

```
batchRender -f "";
```

Result: *An animation is rendered.*

A typical batch rendering sequence amalgamates all of the setup attributes into a few lines. A standard batch code appears like…

```
setAttr defaultRenderGlobals.animation 1;
setAttr defaultRenderGlobals.imageFormat 8;
setAttr "defaultRenderGlobals.startFrame" 5;
setAttr "defaultRenderGlobals.endFrame" 1205;
setAttr "defaultRenderGlobals.byFrameStep" 1;
setAttr "defaultRenderGlobals.extensionPadding" 4;
setAttr defaultResolution.width 1000;
setAttr defaultResolution.height 1000;
batchRender -f "";
```

Result: *An animation of 1000x1000 pixel jpg images starting with frame 5 to 1205 was produced.*

Afterward

This manual is designed to quickly bring non-programmers and designers up to speed with the basics of computational design as well as provide the fundamentals of Maya MEL four-dimensional modeling to veteran programmers. The previous twelve chapters discussed the importance of variables, conditionals, commands and loops, while also revealing primary geometry, sub-geometry, animation and rendering tools. The amount of content is quite expansive, but these chapters consist of only a fraction of the exposed functionality. With practice and use, familiarity of the language will be come second nature and ultimately impact any user's workflow.

Future editions of this manual will cover the following topics:

Abstract Geometry

Generative Capabilities

Advance Rendering Techniques

Detection and Emergence

Time-based Automation

Generative Script-writing and Procedures

Particles

Dynamic Bodies

File Management, Geometric Conversions, and Translators

Mutators

Evolutionary Algorithms

Rationalization and Optimization

Parametric Connections

~

INDEX:

About the Author, Nicholas Pisca.
Nicholas Pisca received his BSAS from the University of Wisconsin Milwaukee School of Architecture and Urban Planning in 2003 and his Master of Architecture from the Southern California Institute of Architecture in 2006. He had focused his undergraduate studies on mathematics, architecture, structural engineering and German, and his graduate academic research on 4D computational design in architectural, web, cinema and other design environments. Computationally, his algorithmic focus consisted primarily of a combination of emergent and evolutionary techniques in Rhinoscript, ActionScript and Maya MEL. His thesis, called Flesh[]logically.transparent++rand[$x], served as a launch pad for his professorial career; he has conducted seminars and workshops at the Southern California Institute of Architecture (SCIarc), University of California Santa Barbara – Media Arts and Technology (UCSB-MAT), the Ohio State University Knowlton School of Architecture, University of Washington-Seattle, Royal Melbourne Institute of Technology Architecture School (RMIT) and various corporate firms. The premiere architectural rationalization services firm Gehry Technologies hired Pisca in 2005, where he became the company's first Automation Consultant. Mastering the language Visual Basic, he developed and instructed automation for advanced Building Information Modeling (BIM) and the parametric programs Digital Project and CATIA. In 2007 he became the Senior Automation Consultant, where he runs various scripting projects for large-scale architectural, contracting, fabrication, and research projects and is editor of the online resource GTWiki. He accepted the position of Lecturer at the University of California Santa Barbara MAT graduate program in 2008. Pisca is the founder of the research firm 0001d, where architectural, web, cinema and multi-media projects and simulations are designed with advanced automation techniques. Pisca also started the meta scripting wiki 0001d BLAST (www.nickpisca.com/BLAST), where MEL, VB, RVB, ActionScript and other languages are documented and cataloged. He also promotes WVO awareness and other environmental causes.